Thirty Days in the Land with Jesus

A Holy Land Devotional

CHARLES H. DYER

D0047964

MOODY PUBLISHERS

CHICAGO

© 2012 by
CHARLES H. DYER

Photo Credits: Day 2 is courtesy of the G. Eric and Edith Matson Photograph Collection in the Library of Congress. All other photographs are used by permission of Charles Dyer, the author.

Edited by Jim Vincent
Interior design: Ragont Design
Cover design: Dugan Design Group
Cover image: Photography by Charles H. Dyer.

ISBN: 978-0-8024-0284-4

Library of Congress Cataloging-in-Publication Data

Dyer, Charles H.
    Thirty days in the land with Jesus : a Holy Land devotional / Charles H. Dyer.
        p. cm.
    Includes bibliographical references.
    ISBN 978-0-8024-0284-4
    1. Jesus Christ—Biography—Meditations. I. Title.
BT306.43.D94 2012
232.9—dc23

                        2011044066

We hope you enjoy this book from Moody Publishers. Our goal is to provide high-quality, thought-provoking books and products that connect truth to your real needs and challenges. For more information on other books and products written and produced from a biblical perspective, go to www.moody publishers.com or write to:

Moody Publishers
820 N. LaSalle Boulevard
Chicago, IL 60610

3 5 7 9 10 8 6 4 2

Printed in the United States of America

Praise for *Thirty Days in the Land with Jesus*

Thirty Days in the Land with Jesus will not only hold a place in my favorite books collection, but it will also be within reach on my bedside table. Second only to being with Charlie on one of his renowned Holy Land tours, this devotional will make you feel as if you are there—and make you want to make the trip.

> —**Jerry B. Jenkins**
> Novelist & Biographer
> Owner, Christian Writers Guild

Few people have a deeper passion for Israel than Dr. Charlie Dyer. It courses through his veins. Yet Charlie's primary goal is not just to introduce people to the land of the Book, as wonderful as that is; it is to increase their love for the Lord of the Book. This thirty-day devotional sets the course for such a journey. Like a tasty appetizer before a fine meal, it whets the taste buds for what is ahead. If you want to maximize your time in Israel, carve out a month before your departure and devour this material. Nothing will prepare you better.

> —**Dr. J. Paul Nyquist**
> President, Moody Bible Institute

If you have never been to Israel, this book will stimulate your imagination. If you have made the journey, it will bring back many memories. For all, *Thirty Days in the Land with Jesus* will take you on a spiritual journey with the One we worship as Savior and Lord.

> —**Dr. Gary Chapman**
> Author and Conference Speaker

Thirty Days in the Land with Jesus is not an ordinary devotional book. Charlie has led thousands to Israel and also trained hundreds of pastors to lead Bible tours. He is able to take the Bible, history, and archaeology and fuse them together into life lessons you'll never forget. Once he explains the Scriptures, you see them in high definition.

Charlie made my Bible come alive the first time I went to Israel, and I've never been the same. So get ready to experience Israel! Your personal tour guide awaits you!

> —**Tom Doyle**
> Vice President, e3 Ministries
> Author of *Two Nations under God*, *Breakthrough*, *Desperation*, and *Dreams and Visions*

If you have always longed to visit Israel but haven't or can't, then this superbly crafted volume supplies the next best way to go. With Dr. Charlie Dyer as your expert guide and in the comfort of your own residence, this spiritual pilgrimage proves to be extremely cost effective and time efficient, not to mention that it can be repeated every month at no extra cost. By the way, for those who have already been there, this must-read volume will wonderfully refresh your precious memories and let you repeatedly relive that once-in-a-lifetime trip.

—**Dr. Richard Mayhue**
Executive Vice President and Dean, The Master's Seminary

Not just a 30-day devotional. Not just a pictorial travel guide. Not just a commentary on the places of Jesus. *Thirty Days in the Land with Jesus* is all three, and more. It's the perfect combination that will allow the land to draw you closer to the Lord.

—**Dr. Woodrow Kroll**
Back to the Bible

There is a saying that once someone has traveled to Israel, they are never the same. Through his multiple trips to the Holy Land, Dr. Charles Dyer knows this to be very true. He now offers us a devotional guide that helps us to see beyond the archeological ruins, the desert towns, and the tourist stops. He invites us to walk with Jesus and to see the land through His eyes. May this book serve to remind those who have traveled to the Holy Land of what a life-changing experience it was to walk where Jesus walked. For those who have yet to go, may this devotional make your heart race just a bit faster in anticipation of visiting the land where world-changing history was made by the Savior from Nazareth.

—**Janet Parshall**
Nationally syndicated talk show host

If you can't go to Israel with Dr. Charlie Dyer, then by all means read this book! I have spent many weeks studying with my dear friend in Israel and know firsthand the impact of his biblical insights and the vast repository of his knowledge about of the land, people, and history of Israel. No one links the Land to God's Word like Charlie does. This book will be a constant reference and companion for every future trip I take. I couldn't recommend a book more highly.

—**Dr. Mark L. Bailey**
President, Dallas Theological Seminary

What a blessing to be taught about the land of the Book and the life and ministry of Jesus Christ in a way that ties two millenniums together! You'll not only visit the sites of Jesus' life and ministry; you will also gain nuggets of truth from Charlie's scholarship and firsthand experience of teaching God's Word where it happened. Because I have taught year after year in Israel and visited these sites, reading this book and seeing the pictures makes me homesick.

—**Kay Arthur**
Author, Teacher, CEO and Cofounder
Precept Ministries International

*To Dan Anderson, Jon Gauger, and
Denny Nugent—three friends and colleagues
who worked so hard to help make
The Land and the Book radio program a reality.
Thank you for your commitment to excellence . . .
and for the passion you share for
the land of Israel and the Word of God!*

Those who trust in the Lord are as Mount Zion,
which cannot be moved, but abides forever.
As the mountains surround Jerusalem, so the Lord
surrounds His people
from this time forth and forever.
Psalm 125:1–2

Contents

Introduction:
Imagine Being There

What would it have been like to travel the roads and pathways of the Promised Land in the footsteps of Jesus? Imagine following the crowds as they gathered on hillsides in Galilee to listen to His messages, or to feast on the loaves and fish He provided. Or picture yourself squeezing past the crowd filling the narrow street outside Peter's house in Capernaum, all waiting to visit with the Great Physician. Or think what it would have been like to stop for a cool, refreshing drink of water by the well in Samaria as Jesus talked with a woman about the living water He could provide. Or imagine listening to hundreds of coins clattering across the temple courtyard as Jesus upended the tables of the money changers.

If you have never visited Israel you might struggle

to place these events into their proper historical and geographical context. You can't seem to make sense of the names of all the people and places you read in the Bible. You can't pronounce the names, and you don't really understand the geographical significance of the places.

So you do the next best thing. You picture the event happening by a location that looks similar to a place with which you *are* familiar.

When you read about events on the *Sea* of Galilee, you might mistakenly picture a much larger body of water—the Atlantic Ocean or Lake Michigan, for example—that fits your mental picture of what a "sea" ought to be. Or when you read of how Israel crossed the Jordan *River* or God commended His Son during Jesus' baptism there, you might substitute the mighty Mississippi . . . or the Colorado . . . or the Columbia, or some other river you think might match the grandeur of the events occurring in the Jordan River.

But reading our geographical understanding into the Bible can lead to a misunderstanding of the story. And that's why so many visitors to the Holy Land experience "aha!" moments—flashes of insight when a particular story of the Bible comes sharply into focus as the pilgrim actually sees the spot where it took place. Mark Twain experienced the same flashes of insight during his visit to the Holy Land, and he quickly realized how much he had misread the Bible prior to his trip.

> I can see easily enough that if I wish to profit by this tour and come to a correct understanding of the matters of interest connected with it, I must studiously and faithfully unlearn a great many things I have somehow absorbed concerning Palestine. I must begin a system of reduction. Like my grapes which the spies bore out of the Promised Land, I have got everything in Palestine on too large a scale. Some of my ideas were wild enough. The word "Palestine" always brought to my mind a vague suggestion of a country as large as the United States. I do not know why, but such was the case. I suppose it was because I could not conceive of a small country having so large a history.[1]

I have two goals for this book. First, I want to guide you in a month-long journey through the land of Israel. If you've already been to the Holy Land, this is an opportunity to relive that adventure. And if you have never visited there, *Thirty Days in the Land with Jesus* will help you experience the journey without the hassle of packing and flying. (Who knows, afterward you may want to begin planning an actual trip so you can turn the beautiful 2D photos in this book into true 3D!) The pictures and descriptions are intended to help you more accurately visualize the land of Israel. The more you are able to place the events in the life of Jesus into their proper historical and geographical context, the more you will understand the message of the Bible.

At the same time, these thirty days will spotlight the life of Jesus in a way that draws you closer to Him. The purpose for this book is not merely to help you understand more accurately the Word of God, as important as that is. Rather, my desire is to help you fall more in love with the God of the Word as you journey through the land with the Son of God.

This book is *not* designed to be read quickly. Instead, over the next month read one chapter each day . . . slowly, deliberately, thoughtfully. Think of it as a thirty-day spiritual journey through the land, walking alongside the Savior. My prayer is that as you encounter Jesus on this journey you will respond as the two disciples who walked and talked with Him on the roadway to Emmaus. "Were not our hearts burning within us while He was speaking to us on the road, while He was explaining the Scriptures to us?" (Luke 24:32).

NOTE

1. Mark Twain, *The Innocents Abroad* (n.p.: American Publishing Company, 1869, repr. CreateSpace/Amazon, 2010), 203.

DAY

1

Swaddling Clothes for a King

For much of the twentieth century in Western society, giving birth was viewed as little more than a medical "procedure." Hospitals. Doctors. Nurses. For a time hospitals wouldn't even allow fathers to be present at birth.

Thankfully, the harsher, clinical atmosphere has softened, and we're again recognizing the birth process as a normal part of life. Birthing rooms in some hospitals offer warm colors; older siblings are sometimes invited to visit, and Mom and Dad can spend some time alone with the newborn in the almost-like-home setting.

When Jesus was born, things were much different. No hospitals. No doctors. No nurses. The Gospel of Luke, written by a medical doctor, describes the event in a simple, natural way. Joseph and Mary had traveled from Nazareth to Bethlehem to register for the required Roman census. "While they were there, the days were completed for her to give birth. And she gave birth to her firstborn son; and she wrapped Him in cloths, and laid Him in a manger, because there was no room for them in the inn" (Luke 2:6–7).

Who helped Mary with the delivery? We're not told, but it's reasonable to assume a midwife or some older women from the town assisted the mother-to-be. Every village must have had a group of wise, experienced women who helped young mothers through the process of delivery. Since both Mary and Joseph traced their family lines back to David, it's reasonable to assume the women of Bethlehem would come to the aid of these out-of-town relatives. There may have been no space available to house the young couple, but these women must surely have had room in their hearts to show compassion to a young woman going through labor and delivery for the first time.

If Joseph followed the custom of the day, he was outside waiting anxiously for news about the condition of his wife and child. Perhaps some of the men from the town were also gathered with him, offering words of encouragement and advice. "I'm sure everything will be fine. Perhaps the child will even be a son!" one might have said, unaware that Joseph already knew the sex of this unborn child! (See Matthew 1:18–21.)

After giving birth, Mary wrapped her newborn son in "cloths," or, as you might remember from the King James Version of the Bible, "swaddling clothes" (Luke 2:7). But why would Mary wrap her son in strips of cloth bound tightly around His body?

Some ancient writers saw the swaddling clothes as a picture of the divine nature being concealed, swaddled as it were, in human flesh. Others saw a typological relationship between Jesus being wrapped in cloths and placed in a manger as a baby and later being "wrapped in a linen cloth" and laid "in a tomb cut into the rock" following His crucifixion (see Luke 23:53).

But could there be a simpler explanation?

In ancient times the wrapping of a child in strips of cloth was a sign of the parents' loving reception of their child. In the Middle East a newborn was bathed in warm salt water and then wrapped in strips of soft, warm fabric. How do we know this? Two Old Testament passages give us insight into these practices.

The first is from the Book of Job. Toward the end of the book God confronted Job and asked Job to explain how God created the world. "Where were you when I laid the foundation of the earth? . . . Or who enclosed the sea with doors when, bursting forth, it went out from the womb; when I made a cloud its garment, *and thick darkness its swaddling band*?" (Job 38:4–9, italics added).

God describes the "birth" of the world, and He pictures the dark clouds swirling around the planet as the strips of cloth He wrapped around this new creation.

If the Book of Job pictures God blessing His new creation by wrapping it in swaddling cloths, the prophet Ezekiel uses the imagery to picture a far sadder scene. He describes the history of the city of Jerusalem as the story of God's compassion toward an unwanted child. The city's origins gave no hint as to its future greatness as Israel's capital and the site of God's holy temple. He writes, "As for your birth, on the day you were born your navel cord was not cut, nor were you washed with water for cleansing; you were not rubbed with salt *or even wrapped in cloths*" (Ezekiel 16:4, italics added).

As an "unwanted child," Jerusalem was neglected and uncared for until God showered His grace on her. But note carefully that wrapping the child in swaddling cloths was part of the normal care and love one would expect at a child's birth.

If all newborns were wrapped in swaddling cloths, in what sense was the wrapping of Jesus in such cloths symbolic? Remember, when the angels appeared to the shepherds, they gave them a sign. "For today in the city of David there has been born for you a Savior, who is Christ the Lord. This will be a sign for you: you will find a baby wrapped in cloths and lying in a manger" (Luke 2:11–12).

The key here is to note that the swaddling cloths by themselves are *not* the sign. The shepherds would find the child wrapped in swaddling cloths *and* lying in a manger. The likelihood of both events happening randomly was extremely remote. A toddler could conceivably climb into a feeding trough, but a child wrapped tightly in swaddling bands (as a newborn would be) could only be placed there deliberately. And what mother would place her newborn into the equivalent of a barnyard feeding trough? That's

A stone manger, or feeding trough, from Megiddo

how the shepherds would know they had found *the* child.

A newborn king—even the Jewish Messiah—wrapped in swaddling cloths? That wouldn't be unusual. The cut of the cloth and style of fabric might have differed, but whether the newborn child was the son of a prince or a pauper, one would expect to find him swaddled.

But a newborn child—especially a king—being deliberately placed in a manger, a common feeding trough for animals? That certainly made it easy for these shepherds to search through the village until they found the child whose birth had just been announced. And yet, I wonder what was going through their minds as they started on their scavenger hunt, searching for the King of the Jews in a barnyard manger.

In many ways things haven't changed. People today still struggle to accept Jesus as the Messiah, or as the Son of God, or as their personal Savior, because He doesn't match their preconceived ideas. But God asks us, just as the angels did the shepherds, to look beyond expectations and focus on the facts. One doesn't expect to find a newborn king in a manger, but this one was. That was the sign. And one doesn't expect God's Son, the Messiah, to die on a cross, but this one did . . . to pay the price for our sins.

And maybe that's what makes Jesus Himself such an amazing gift from God. "For God so loved the world, that He gave His only begotten Son, that whoever believes in

Him shall not perish, but have eternal life" (John 3:16).

DO YOU HAVE A PERSONAL
relationship with the Jesus of the Bible? Do you
know the One who was born in Bethlehem, who died
on a cross in Jerusalem to pay the penalty for your
sin, who rose from a borrowed tomb three days later,
who ascended to heaven, and who is coming back
again? If not, why not begin your thirty-day journey of
discovery by coming to know this one about whom
God said, "This is My beloved Son, in whom I am
well-pleased" (Matthew 3:17)?

Read through the Gospel of Luke to learn what
God says about this one called Jesus. And perhaps,
like those shepherds so long ago, you will find yourself "glorifying and praising God for all that they had
heard and seen, just as had been told them"
(Luke 2:20).

DAY 2

Wise Men from Where?

Today might not be Christmas, but since when does the Christmas story need to be limited to December 25? In fact, although the Western church celebrates Jesus' birth on that date, we don't know the exact day He was born. The earliest reference to His birth being on December 25 was written a few centuries *after* the time of Christ. And while this could be the correct date, we simply can't be sure.

One thing we *do* know, however, is that the presents for Jesus never arrived on the day He was born. To understand why, let's go back to Bethlehem and look more closely at the details of His birth.

On the night Jesus was born, a heavenly host of angels blasted away the darkness to announce His birth to the shepherds. They went to Bethlehem to find the baby, who was swaddled in strips of cloth and lying in a manger. Early church tradition places the manger in a cave, and that does make good sense. Bethlehem is located in the limestone hills that form the mountainous backbone of Judea. Thousands of natural caves dot the hillsides in the region, and many are used as sheepfolds. It's easy to imagine a homeowner in Bethlehem using the cave just outside his house as a shelter for his animals.

Eight days after His birth the baby was circumcised and named Jesus, *Yeshua*—the Hebrew name Joshua, which means "the Lord is salvation." Forty days after His birth, Joseph and Mary made the five-mile journey to Jerusalem with their infant son, "to present Him to the Lord" as Luke describes it in 2:22. They made this trip in strict obedience to the Law of Moses, fulfilling the command given in Leviticus 12.

The fact that they offered "a pair of turtledoves or two young pigeons" (Luke 2:24) tells us something of the financial condition of this young family. You see, the Law said the woman was to bring "a one year old lamb for a burnt offering and a young pigeon or a turtledove for a sin offering" (Leviticus 12:6). But then it made allowance for those without the financial means to do so. "But if she cannot afford a lamb, then she shall take two turtledoves or two young pigeons" (v. 8). Joseph and Mary couldn't afford the cost of a lamb.

The Gospel of Matthew picks up the account of Jesus' birth from this point. Mary and Joseph must have traveled back to Bethlehem and resided there for some time. Herod was still ruling as king, though the end of his despotic reign was drawing near. Somehow the birth of this rival king had escaped his notice. That is, until a caravan of wise men rode into Jerusalem.

Tradition has fixed the number of wise men at three, and even supplied us with their names: Caspar, Melchior,

The arrival of the magi at Bethlehem (from the G. Eric and Edith Matson Photograph Collection in the Library of Congress)

and Balthasar. But the Bible tells us neither the number of wise men nor their names. What the Bible *does* tell us, however, is quite revealing. Matthew describes these travelers as "magi from the east," and this has led to much speculation. Some believe these travelers were from Babylon and trace their interest in the birth of the Messiah back to the time of Daniel, who was placed in charge of the wise men of Babylon (Daniel 2:48).

Others see in the word "magi" links to the Persians from what is now called Iran. Magi were the priestly caste of the Persian Zoroastrian religion. They paid particular attention to astronomy and astrology. Certainly they would have noticed an unusual—and unexpected—star in the sky. But I'm not sure if we can read too much into their identification based on this one word because the same Greek word, *magos,* is used elsewhere to describe a Jewish sorcerer and false prophet on the island of Cyprus during the time of Paul (Acts 13:6–8). The word seems to describe individuals known for their wisdom or ability to ferret out knowledge, whether through a God-given ability (like Daniel), or through occult activity, astrology, or interpreting dreams. It was used to describe people from Persia, Babylon, and even this Jewish false prophet on Cyprus.

There is a third possibility for the identity of the wise men, one that's not as well known. These wise men would also have lived to the east of Judah, but not as far to the east as Babylon or Persia. It's possible that these wise men were *sheikhs*, Arab princes of the desert who came to find the Messiah. The possibility isn't as far-fetched as it might first seem.

The Book of Isaiah includes a fascinating prediction, often overlooked in the midst of the other amazing prophecies in that book. In Isaiah 60, the prophet writes, "Arise, shine; for your light has come, and the glory of the Lord has risen upon you. . . . *The wealth of the nations will come to you. A multitude of camels will cover you, the young camels of Midian and Ephah; all those from Sheba will come; they will bring gold and frankincense, and will bear good news of the praises of the Lord*" (Isaiah 60:1–6, italics added).

A light will shine and men will come on camels from the Arab kingdoms to the east bearing gold and frankincense. Sound familiar? The groups named by Isaiah are Arab tribes from the Arabian Peninsula. Imagine, Arabs coming to celebrate the arrival of the Jewish Messiah!

But let's return to the last of the events surrounding Christ's birth.

Herod—and everyone else in Jerusalem—must not have seen the star when it first appeared at the time of Christ's birth, but these wise men had. After their meeting with Herod, the star *reappeared* to the wise men and "stood over" the house in Bethlehem to which it led them. Think about that for a second. This must have been more than just a mere star, planet, meteor, or comet. Such heavenly bodies could point you in a general direction, but they couldn't identify a specific house in a small village.

So what was the star?

Could the original sign in the sky have been the angelic choir in Luke 2 that appeared to the shepherds? No one in Jerusalem bothered to look to the sky that night when "an angel of the Lord suddenly stood before them, and the glory of the Lord shone around them" (v. 9). As bright as God's glory was accompanying this angel, imagine what happened when "suddenly there appeared with the angel a multitude of the heavenly host" (v. 13). The glow in the sky must have been visible for miles, perhaps for hundreds of miles. Could this be what the wise men saw that first night? Certainly it's possible. And the reappearance of this angel could be the "star" that guided the wise men to Bethlehem, and to the very house where Jesus and His parents were staying.

Significantly, the wise men found Jesus and His parents living in a house, not a stable (Matthew 2:11). Months have passed since the time of Jesus' birth. Perhaps some of the many people who had come to Bethlehem to be registered in the census had now gone home. Or perhaps some family in the town had pity on this poor couple with the new baby and made room for them in their home. But for whatever reason, Mary, Joseph, and Jesus are now in more comfortable surroundings. But only for a little while longer.

The wise men must have departed from Herod in the late afternoon or early evening. And Herod carefully calculated how long it would take for these wise men to accomplish his bidding. Two hours or less to ride to Bethlehem (just a five-mile journey). An hour or so to search the village for the child. Perhaps it would be too late to return to Jerusalem that night, but they should definitely be reporting back early the next day.

The wise men and Joseph must have had their separate dreams that very same night. Joseph and Mary left early the next morning, fleeing toward Egypt, while the wise men hastily sought another roadway back toward the east—one that avoided Jerusalem. How long did Herod wait before sending his soldiers to Bethlehem? Knowing Herod, not too long!

AND THAT BRINGS US BACK TO

Mary, Joseph, and Jesus . . . to Jesus' Christmas gifts . . . and to us. How could a family so poor that it couldn't even afford the normal sacrifice for a newborn son ever hope to get away from someone as powerful as Herod the Great? Fleeing to Egypt was as daunting a journey for them as running away to a far off country halfway around the world would be for us today.

But remember Isaiah's prophecy . . . and Matthew's record of its fulfillment. "The wealth of the nations will come to you. . . . they will bring gold and frankincense" (Isaiah 60:5–6). Indeed, the magi "presented to Him gifts of gold, frankincense, and myrrh" (Matthew 2:11). God's provision—His "Christmas present"—arrived right on time!

So what does the future hold for you? Our world seems to be facing uncertain times. But pause and remember that God knows your every need. The God who took care of Mary, Joseph, and Jesus is the God who has also promised to take care of you.

DAY 3

A Photograph of Jesus in the Temple

I'm not sure if it was Erma Bombeck, Chuck Swindoll, or some other creative wordsmith who first wrote, "Grandchildren are God's reward for not killing your kids." But whoever it was, they were right! My wife and I don't live near our grandkids, so we look forward to seeing the pictures and videos our son and daughter-in-law post on the Internet. (Hint to Ben and Kelly . . . more pictures!)

I believe most of us like viewing pictures of children, especially if the kids belong to family members or close friends. And that's, in part, why we like the snapshots of baby Jesus we find in the Bible. But such pictures, as precious as they are, are rather rare. We see Jesus as a newborn in a manger surrounded by shepherds in Luke 2. And we see the infant Jesus surrounded by kings from the east presenting Him with presents in Matthew 2.

There are two other, lesser-known photos of Jesus as a child that share a common theme. Both were taken in the temple in Jerusalem. The first is a picture of Jesus taken about six weeks after His birth. In this photo we see Jesus cradled in the arms of an old man as a startled Mary and Joseph look on. Next to them stands an elderly woman. We might assume at first that these are His grandparents, but on the back of the photo someone has written their names. The man is Simeon, and the woman is a prophetess named Anna.

The final picture in Jesus' childhood photo album is taken twelve years later. It's also an image of young Jesus in the temple. Let's look at this photo, also described in Luke 2, more carefully.

Several details in the background stand out. It's spring, just after Passover, and the mountains in the distance are covered in green, while patches of red poppies freckle the hillsides. In the foreground we can see that the crowds of people in the temple have begun to thin out, though many people are still milling around.

For a moment, our attention shifts from the people to the buildings. The photograph features the Court of the Gentiles, the large outer plaza surrounding the temple proper. On the left side of the photo are several limestone columns extending upward beyond the top of the picture. Just beyond the row of columns we see the broad, open courtyard. The photographer must have stood in the royal stoa, sometimes called the portico of Solomon, because of the size and grandeur of this veritable forest of limestone columns. In reality, this amazing covered portico—and virtually everything else in the temple standing before us—was built by Herod the Great, not Solomon. It's a paradox that something so magnificent could have been built by someone so evil.

Turning back to the people in the photo, we note

Portico of Solomon in the model of the second temple in Jerusalem

young Jesus. He just turned twelve, the age when He was considered to be a man—responsible for His own actions and decisions. We're not sure if Judah had formal bar mitzvahs in Jesus' day, but the concept behind them was certainly in place.

The next group we notice is the rabbis. These teachers of the Law add a sense of dignity and gravitas to the photo. They know God's Word and are in the temple to teach it to their disciples and to all others who stop to listen.

Finally, we spot Joseph and Mary. Why hadn't we noticed them before? Perhaps it's because they don't look the same as they did in the previous photos. Granted, they're twelve years older, but that's not it. In the previous pictures they were smiling, but in this one they're not. They almost appear to be angry . . . or worried . . . or deeply distressed.

A note on the back of the photo explains the problem. "Left Jerusalem after Passover. Thought Jesus was with His friends in our group. Didn't realize He wasn't with us till after the first full day. Returned to Jerusalem and searched for a full day before finding Him in the temple." Now the expression on their faces makes sense. It's the look of parents whose child had gone missing for several days—a look of anguish, anxiety, and anger. They were relieved to find Him, and angry at Him for causing them such stress and fright.

Evidently, for the past three days—days of traveling away from, then back to, Jerusalem, along with the additional day of frantic searching in the city itself—Jesus had been "sitting in the midst of the teachers, both listening to them and asking them questions." And the rabbis had been impressed with this young lad. "And all who heard Him were amazed at His understanding and His answers." (See Luke 2:46–47.) Of course, the teachers had no idea they were talking to the *Author* of the Book they had spent their lives studying!

Jesus' response to His parents must have surprised them. "Why is it that you were looking for Me? Did you not know that I had to be in My Father's house?" (v. 49). Even at the young age of twelve Jesus had full knowledge of His relationship to God. His earthly parents didn't understand, even as we struggle to understand, how the eternal God could have come to earth in a human body, to be standing in front of them as a young boy.

As the account ends, Jesus places Himself back under the authority of His earthly parents. He goes home with them and "continued in subjection to them" (v. 51). Mary remembers the incident . . . and later shares this touching story with Dr. Luke.

WHAT CAN WE LEARN FROM THIS
time in the temple with young Jesus? Perhaps it's
this: Even the Son of God put Himself under the
authority of others. He asked questions of the aged
rabbis, and He willingly followed His parents back to
Nazareth. In an age when we're told to demand our
personal freedom and liberty—to focus on our
rights—Jesus was willing to submit. And if the divine
Son of God was willing to place Himself under the authority of others, shouldn't we be willing to do the
same?

The apostle Paul addressed this very issue when
he wrote to the church in Philippi and pointed to
Jesus as our ultimate example. "Have this attitude in
yourselves which was also in Christ Jesus, who,
although He existed in the form of God, did not regard
equality with God a thing to be grasped, but emptied
Himself, taking the form of a bond-servant, and being
made in the likeness of men. Being found in appearance as a man, He humbled Himself by becoming
obedient to the point of death, even death on a cross"
(Philippians 2:5–8).

Are you struggling to obey those God has placed in authority over you? It might be your boss at work, the leadership in your church, or those in charge of our government. Rather than demanding our rights and pushing against that authority, like Christ we should be willing to give up our right to demand our own way and to submit. Is this difficult? Absolutely. Can it be done? Look again at the photograph of Jesus in the temple. He listened to the rabbis, even though He knew His Word better than they. And He obeyed His earthly parents, even when He understood His relationship to His true heavenly Father. Let's see if, today, we can get the photograph of our lives to match that of Jesus in the temple!

DAY 4

The Puzzling Prophecy: A Messiah from Shoot Town

I n his remarkable gospel account, the apostle John provides an intimate portrait of the first disciples called by Jesus. The encounter took placed near Jericho, just after His baptism, as Jesus prepared to journey to Galilee. Jesus first called Andrew and another individual—whom most assume to be John himself—as His first disciples. Andrew then searched out his brother, Simon Peter, and brought him to the Messiah. The next day Jesus summoned another man named Philip to follow Him as one of His disciples. He commanded, and Philip obeyed.

Philip was from Bethsaida, the same hometown as Andrew and Peter, and he followed in Andrew's footsteps and went looking for someone else to bring to Jesus. He found Nathanael who was from Cana in Galilee—the region that included Nazareth—and told him, "We have found Him of whom Moses in the Law and also the Prophets wrote—Jesus of Nazareth, the son of Joseph" (John 1:45).

The moment Phillip said the Messiah was from Nazareth, Nathanael had serious doubts. "Nazareth!" he snorted. "Can any good thing come out of Nazareth?" (John 1:46). Nathanael's skepticism was grounded in his very practical knowledge of the region. Nazareth was *not* a major town. It *didn't* sit astride a major road through the country. It had *not* played a significant role in the nation's history. As a result, it was certainly not the spot where one would expect to find Israel's Messiah.

But why was Nazareth so invisible throughout Israel's history? The answer rests, in large measure, on its geography.

If you would stand atop the Mount of Precipice along the southern edge of the ridge on which Nazareth sits, you'd better understand Nathanael's skepticism. The little village of Nazareth sat in a bowl-shaped depression just beyond the edge of the ridge. From the Mount of Precipice one can look down into this depression and imagine a tiny hamlet ringed on all sides by hills. One had to climb up the steep ridge—and then walk back down into the valley—to reach Nazareth.

The International Highway—that ancient thoroughfare that extended from Mesopotamia through the land of Judea to Egypt—passed through the Jezreel Valley just a few miles to the south of Nazareth. So close . . . and yet so far away. Only those with business in Nazareth would turn off that highway to make the difficult climb up the Nazareth Ridge and then down the other side into the secluded valley where the village sat.

How difficult was the roadway up to Nazareth? In 1867 Mark Twain made the journey *down* the road from Nazareth to the Jezreel Valley on horseback. In *The Innocents Abroad*, he described his journey this way, "We dismounted and drove the horses down a bridle path which I think was fully as crooked as a corkscrew, which I know to be as steep as the downward sweep of a rainbow, and which I believe to be the worst piece of road in the geography except one in the Sandwich Islands, which I remember painfully, and possibly one or two mountain trails in the Sierra Nevadas."[1] Evidently, he didn't think much of the road to Nazareth—and he was traveling downhill!

Nathanael knew his geography—and his history—when he asked if anything good could come from Nazareth. More importantly, he also knew current Jewish thinking about the promised Messiah. From a Jewish perspective, when the Messiah would come He would be born in Bethlehem and revealed in Jerusalem. Bethlehem was the city of David, Israel's first great king in the promised line. And Jerusalem was where the temple was located, where the religious leadership was centered, and the city from which the Messiah would someday reign. But Nazareth? How could anyone of significance possibly come from a place as *insignificant* as Nazareth! Nathanael was sincere, but in this case he was sincerely wrong.

Let's not be too hard on Nathanael. We also associate size with importance, and we also judge based on appearance and background. It's hard for us to imagine someone great coming from a place that is small, or remote, or insignificant. Did you watch the YouTube clip of forty-seven-year-old Susan Boyle standing in front of the judges on the television program *Britain's Got Talent*? The audience laughed at this slightly frumpy lady from a small town—that is until she opened her mouth to sing "I Dreamed a Dream" from *Les Misérables*!

The amazing transformation from skepticism to awe and wonder expressed by the audience listening to Susan Boyle is the same transformation that took place in Nathanael. This one who wondered how anything good could come from Nazareth, when confronted with a demonstration of Jesus' omniscience, immediately responded, "Rabbi, You are the Son of God; You are the King of Israel" (John 1:49). Something infinitely good *could* come from Nazareth.

Jesus had been born in Bethlehem—just as the prophet Micah predicted. But if He was the Messiah—and indeed He was!—why did He grow up in Nazareth? This village was God's perfect choice for two reasons. First, it was secluded. As such it provided a safe, protected place where Jesus could grow in wisdom and stature and favor with God and men (see Luke 2:52), away from the prying eyes

Netzer, the shoots or branches growing from the roots of an olive tree

and political plotting of those in power who were threatened by any potential rival. Joseph, Mary, and Jesus returned to Judea after hiding in Egypt to escape Herod. After King Herod died, however, his son had taken his place, so the family headed north to Nazareth instead. Nazareth was secluded and remote, a perfect place to remain concealed until it was God's time for the Messiah to be revealed.

But there appears to be a second reason God wanted His Messiah to come from Nazareth. God chose *this* specific village to fulfill one additional prophetic sign concerning the Messiah. Matthew tells us in his Gospel that Joseph, Mary, and Jesus "came and lived in a city called Nazareth. This was to fulfill what was spoken through the prophets: 'He shall be called a Nazarene'" (Matthew 2:23).

According to Matthew, Jesus' connection to the village of Nazareth was predicted by more than one prophet—it was the *prophets* (plural) who foretold the Messiah would be "called a Nazarene." But where is that prophecy in the Old Testament, and why didn't Nathanael remember it?

Perhaps the answer to this riddle lies in the name itself. "Nazareth" comes from the Hebrew word *netzer*, a word meaning "shoot" or "branch." The *netzer* is the shoot that grows from the root of the olive tree . . . and it can eventually become another trunk of the tree jutting out from the base. The word *netzer*, along with another word for branch, was used by the Old Testament prophets Isaiah, Jeremiah, and Zechariah to refer to the Messiah. Isaiah wrote, "Then a shoot [*netzer*] will spring from the stem of Jesse, and a branch from his roots will bear fruit" (11:1). Jeremiah also spoke of the time when God would "raise up for David a righteous Branch; and He will reign as king and act wisely and do justice and righteousness in the land" (23:5). And through the prophet Zechariah God announced, "I am going to bring in My servant the Branch" (3:8).

The "*netzer* from the stem of Jesse," the "Branch," would grow to become God's Messiah. Three different Old Testament prophets made this prediction.

How would Israel recognize her Messiah? Certainly He would need to be from the line of David. Obviously He had to be born in Bethlehem. But I believe Matthew adds one final piece to the puzzle. The Messiah also needed to be the *netzer*, the shoot. And how better to have that fulfilled than to have Him grow up in "shoot town"— *Nazareth*! This small detail was just one more piece of the puzzle to validate Jesus' claim to be the Messiah.

And that brings us back to this seemingly insignificant village. Nazareth was small and located off the beaten path. "Can any good thing come out of Nazareth?" asked Nathanael.

NOTE

1. Mark Twain, *The Innocents Abroad* (n.p.: American Publishing

BUT *NOTHING* IS INSIGNIFICANT
if it's part of God's plan. This tiny town, with its
prophetic name, was the boyhood home of God's
incarnate Son and Israel's promised Messiah. You
see, God delights in using the seemingly insignificant
things of this world to display the greatness of His
plan. The apostle Paul said something very similar in
1 Corinthians 1. "But God has chosen the foolish
things of the world to shame the wise, and God has
chosen the weak things of the world to shame the
things which are strong, and the base things of the
world and the despised . . . so that no man may boast
before God" (vv. 27–29).

Do you struggle with feelings of insignificance?
Have you ever felt your life just wasn't that important? Have you ever wondered how God could use
someone like you, someone with your limitations and
struggles? If so, walk with me back to the top of the
Nazareth Ridge, and look down at the village that was
once home to Israel's Messiah. *Nothing* is insignificant if it is part of God's plan. It doesn't matter where
you're *from*. What matters, and what gives you significance today, is where you're *going*.

DAY 5

Jesus in the Wilderness

After more than seventy-five trips to Israel, I still find the Sea of Galilee amazing and Jerusalem a special place. But my favorite part of Israel is the Judean Wilderness. Really. I find it difficult to explain why. Perhaps it's because it looks today much like it looked in the time of Abraham . . . or Joshua . . . or David . . . or Jesus. It's easy for me to visualize the great men and women of the Bible acting out their part in God's heavenly drama on this stark stage.

Or perhaps I fell in love with the Judean Wilderness because of its subtle transformations. Depending on the time of day, the hilltops can change color from stark white to a light golden brown. In the summer the hills look absolutely barren and desolate, but let the winter rains fall and they turn a pale shade of green as previously unseen grass pushes its way to the surface. Soon splashes of crimson poppies and yellow wildflowers punctuate this emerald carpet. Even the rocks that cover the ground show great variety, if one stops to look carefully. The soft, white chalk is mixed with hard pieces of limestone. In other places entire hillsides are covered with a mixture of black and brown flint, scattered about in small pieces as if a giant slab had been dropped and shattered.

I fell in love with the Judean Wilderness when I spent an entire day hiking from Jerusalem to Jericho on my very first visit to Israel. I sloshed through a pool of water that seemed to flow out of barren ground, watched a shepherdess eye us in bemused silence as we hiked past her small flock of goats, and felt thirst when the last of the water from my two canteens was gone. I saw how flint cuts into the bottom of hiking boots and understood firsthand the intensity of the sun in that part of the world. In short, I bonded with the wilderness and came to understand why in the Bible it symbolizes both the place of testing and the place where God showed Himself to be sufficient for our needs.

It's no accident that Jesus, following His baptism, was led into the wilderness to be tested. Jesus was baptized at a spot on the eastern side of the Jordan River, just across from Jericho. And the wilderness where He went following His baptism was almost certainly the Judean Wilderness that stretches out between Jericho and Jerusalem, and all along the Dead Sea. The traditional Mount of Temptation rises up just behind Jericho. And while we don't know if that's the exact spot where Jesus was tempted, it does mark the general area.

Having spent just one day walking in the wilderness, I struggle to visualize what it would have been like for Jesus to spend forty days and nights in that place. We're not told if it was in the winter or summer, but both would

The Judean Wilderness between Jerusalem and Jericho

be difficult. In the summer the daytime temperature can soar to over a hundred degrees with little shade; while in the winter the cloudless skies allow any daytime warmth to radiate away, leaving a bone-chilling cold at night. The rock-strewn hills and sheer cliffs make walking extremely perilous.

Exhausted. Weak. Hungry. Alone. In His humanity, Jesus was put to the ultimate test in the wilderness. And it was *after* His enduring these extreme conditions for "forty days and forty nights" (Matthew 4:2) that the Devil came to try to break Jesus' dependence on His heavenly Father. Each of Satan's three tests was unique, and yet there's a common theme . . . and a common response. Let's stand off to the side and watch this cosmic confrontation unfold.

Satan first appealed to Jesus' physical needs. Because Jesus had fasted for forty days, Satan focused on the natural human desire for self-preservation. "If You are the Son of God, command that these stones become bread" (Matthew 4:3). In the Greek, the question is not written in a way that implies doubt. A better translation might be "*Since* you are the Son of God. . . ." Satan doesn't doubt Jesus' real identity as God's Son. Rather, Satan tempts Jesus to *use* His power as the Son of God to satisfy His own physical needs. Pointing to the stones covering the face of the ground, Satan encourages Jesus to transform these stones into bread.

But why would it be wrong for Jesus to use His power to make food for Himself? Two details supply us with the answer. First, we're told in verse 1 that Jesus was "led up by the Spirit into the wilderness." His hunger and thirst were part of God's plan for His life at this time. Satan was tempting Jesus to use His own ability to short-circuit God's plan—to take the easy way out. Second, Jesus showed He understood God had a larger plan that can sometimes involve personal sacrifice when He quotes Deuteronomy 8:3. In that passage Moses told Israel that God led them into the wilderness for forty years to humble them and to test them. God caused them to hunger and then fed them with manna to teach them "that man does not live by bread alone, but man lives by everything that proceeds out of the mouth of the LORD." Obedience and humble submission to God might sometimes involve temporary hardship, but those times are designed to help remind us that obedience to God's Word is more important than personal comfort.

For the second part of his plan, Satan transported Jesus to the highest spot on the temple in Jerusalem. "If You are the Son of God, throw Yourself down" (Matthew 4:6). Again, Satan was not casting doubt on Jesus' position as God's Son. Rather, he tempted Jesus to demonstrate He was God's Son by putting Himself in a place where God would have to act in a dramatic fashion to protect Him. To bolster the test, Satan even quotes Scripture, using Psalm 91 to remind Jesus that God had promised to protect Him from harm. And no doubt God would have fulfilled His Word of promise had Jesus jumped.

But that was the subtle intent in Satan's temptation. Could he get Jesus to presume on His relationship to God the Father by forcing the Father to do what Jesus wanted? Today, we do this all the time. Have you ever heard the expression, "It's easier to ask forgiveness than permission"?

Satan was trying to drive a wedge between Jesus and His heavenly Father. But Jesus went back to Scripture to refute Satan's temptation, this time quoting from Deuteronomy 6:16. Though God would have intervened to help His Son had He jumped, Jesus knew it would be wrong to presume on God in this way. "You shall not put the Lord your God to the test." In its original context this command was in connection with God's prohibition against following other gods and thus disobeying the clear commands of the God of Israel.

Satan tried one final time to tempt Jesus. Taking Him to a high mountain, Satan showed Jesus all the kingdoms of the world. Jesus was destined to rule all these kingdoms, but the pathway to that ultimate destiny ran through Calvary. Satan offered Jesus a shortcut to success, a way to achieve all the glory without going through any of the agony. All Jesus had to do was switch allegiances. "All these things I will give You, if you fall down and worship me" (Matthew 4:9). Jesus turned to Deuteronomy a third time to give His answer. "Go, Satan! For it is written, 'You shall worship the Lord your God, and serve Him only'" (Matthew 4:10, quoting Deuteronomy 6:13). In its context this was a clear command that God, and God alone, was the One to be followed and obeyed.

The pathway Jesus had to follow through the wilderness was more difficult and more perilous, but it was the pathway marked out by God. Satan tried to divert Jesus by appealing to the lust of the flesh (put your own physical needs ahead of following God), the pride of life (force God to show people how important you really are), and the lust of the eye (receive all the glory of the kingdoms without going through the agony of the cross by just cutting corners).

WHAT WILDERNESS ARE YOU going through today? Is Satan nearby, whispering in your ear, seeking to short-circuit the time of testing God is taking you through? Don't fall for Satan's subtle traps. Instead, obey God and stay true to His Word. And when the test is over, you will know first-hand that the wilderness is not just a place of testing. It's also the place where God will meet your every need!

DAY
6

The Hometown Boy

O nce again we're standing at the Mount of Precipice on the edge of the Nazareth Ridge. It's an unusually clear day, and we have a magnificent view in all directions. To the north is the city of Nazareth itself. No longer a small village at the bottom of a shallow valley, Nazareth today extends up the hillsides and over the top of the ridgeline on every side.

Turn to the east and there's Mount Tabor with the village of Daburiya—named for the prophetess Deborah—guarding its base. A little further to the south is the Hill of Moreh with the village of Nain clearly visible on the hillside. This is the town where Jesus raised to life a widow's son. And beyond Moreh in the distance is Mount Gilboa, where Gideon chose his three hundred men.

As we turn toward the southwest, we see Mount Carmel stretching toward the Mediterranean Sea. A monastery marks the location of Elijah's conflict with the prophets of Baal, a barely visible dot of white on the mount's summit. Standing here in this one spot, we can literally look over the physical—and spiritual—mountain peaks that define much of Israel's history.

Let's turn back and gaze down at modern Nazareth. In Jesus' day it was just a small village. And yet this village had a synagogue, and Luke 4 records the story of Jesus returning to Nazareth to speak in that synagogue. His fame had begun to spread throughout Galilee. The people of Nazareth had heard stories about this miracle worker who had grown up in their midst. They were excited to hear what He had done, and eager to have Him back in their synagogue sharing from the Word of God.

The attendant handed Jesus the scroll of the prophet Isaiah. Opening it to the portion we know as Isaiah 61, Jesus began to read Isaiah's prophetic message. We don't know if this passage was assigned to be read that day or whether Jesus selected it Himself, but we do know He read a short portion of the text—less than two verses in our Bibles—before closing up the scroll and handing it back to the attendant. What was the passage? "The Spirit of the Lord is upon Me, because He anointed Me to preach the gospel to the poor. He has sent Me to proclaim release to the captives, and recovery of sight to the blind, to set free those who are oppressed, to proclaim the favorable year of the Lord" (Luke 4:18–19).

Every eye in that small synagogue must have been focused intently on Him, wondering what He would do next. Would He deliver one of His already-famous messages? Would He begin healing the many sick and suffering? Certainly the synagogue seemed to have more than

Replica of a New Testament synagogue at Nazareth Village

the usual number of such people that day!

Jesus broke the silence with words that were simple, yet dramatic, "Today this Scripture has been fulfilled in your hearing" (Luke 4:21).

The crowd's initial response was positive. They sensed His words were gracious, perhaps prophetic. Certainly Jesus said that today these very words were being fulfilled in the city of Nazareth. But the crowd's initial impression quickly soured when Jesus exposed the real motive behind all their excitement. "No doubt you will quote this proverb to Me; 'Physician, heal yourself! Whatever we heard was done at Capernaum, do here in your hometown as well'" (Luke 4:23). It seems the people weren't really focused on the message, they were waiting for the miracles!

Jesus then drove home the truth of His statement with two illustrations taken from the same general geographical area. It's almost as if He mentally turned His back on Nazareth to gaze south across the Jezreel Valley, where two other great prophets walked in Old Testament times—Elijah and Elisha. Jesus brought up an uncomfortable truth from the lives of both prophets to reveal the real heart problem that needed healing in Nazareth.

Many Jewish widows were starving in Elijah's day, but the only widow to whom he was sent was a Gentile. And many Jewish people were afflicted with leprosy in

Elisha's day, but the only person he healed of leprosy was a Gentile. What's Jesus' point in using these two illustrations? First, He used them to expose the crowd's improper motives for wanting Him in town. They were there for the *miracles*, not the *message*. Forget the long sermon; just show me the free food and physical healing!

Second, He exposed their prejudice against those who were not of their nationality or religion. They were happy with Jesus as long as He came to heal *their* broken bodies. But squandering God's blessings on Gentiles? On people who worshiped other gods? Such a thought was repugnant to them. They hated the thought—and the One who dared suggest it.

The people got so angry they dragged Jesus out of the synagogue. And that brings us back to the Mount of Precipice on the edge of the Nazareth Ridge. Standing at this spot helps bring the anger of the people into sharper focus. We're standing over a mile from the center of the village, where the synagogue must have been. Yet Luke records that the people drove Jesus "out of the city and . . . to the brow of the hill on which their city had been built, in order to throw Him down the cliff" (Luke 4:29). This is not simply a matter of some angry people escorting Jesus out of the synagogue and walking a few steps to reach the edge of the village. The sheer distance they traveled paints for us a picture of a hostile mob pushing and shoving Jesus out of the synagogue, out of the village itself, and then an additional mile uphill to the edge of the cliff. They intended to push Him off the cliff to His death.

Miraculously, Jesus was able to walk right through the crowd and go on His way. How was He able to do this? We're not told. And frankly, that's not the key point of the story. The major issue is the reality that the hearts of the people of Nazareth were as small as the village itself. At first they were happy to see Jesus, but only because of the miracles they hoped He would perform for them. They missed the significance of His message—that He was the Messiah who had come to fulfill God's prophetic Word. And they had lost sight of the greater truth that the Messiah—and the nation of Israel—had been called to be a light to the Gentiles.

AS WE TURN FROM NAZARETH
and begin the hike down the steep path into the
Jezreel Valley, what lesson can we carry with us in
our spiritual knapsack? Perhaps the most significant
lesson as followers of Christ is to make sure we don't
forget why God has placed us here on earth. Just as
God called Israel to be a light to the Gentiles, so He
has called us to make disciples of all nations. It's not
about the miracles we expect God to give *to* us, it's
about the service He expects to receive *from* us.

In his 1960 inaugural speech President John F.
Kennedy uttered those famous words, "Ask not what
your country can do for you—ask what you can do
for your country." Let's rephrase that line for today.
"Stop focusing on what you want God to do for you;
and focus instead on what you ought to be doing for
Him."

DAY 7

Mount Gerizim— Not Where, But How

Over the years I've taken a number of student groups to Israel. I refer to those trips as peanut-butter-and-jelly tours. They were short on creature comforts but long on firsthand, boots-on-the-ground exploration of the land. These young and active students explored places few "normal" tourists ever go.

The students came to see as much of the land as possible. But sometimes the political situation in Israel forced us to be creative in planning some portions of a trip. Over the years I had developed a friendship with a Muslim shopkeeper in the Old City of Jerusalem. During one of our trips, when the West Bank was closed to regular tourism, the shopkeeper offered to take our students there in a rented Palestinian bus.

For the students who went on this optional, one-day field trip, the experience was priceless. We climbed down the circular staircase at the pool of Gibeon and hiked to the ruins of Ai to relive Joshua's taking of the town. We also visited Bethel, Shechem, Mount Gerizim, and the ancient Israelite capital of Samaria. There were a few tense moments on that trip, but that's when the shopkeeper would jump off the bus and shout to the gathering crowd, who then smiled—and opened their shops. I'm not sure what he said, but I think he must have shouted, "Don't worry. They're just tourists . . . with money!"

Visiting all those sites was great, but the highlight of that trip for the group was our visit to Jacob's well. Imagine visiting a well that was originally dug by Jacob 3,800 years ago. And we could still draw water from that well! We paused to remember a time when the well's most famous visitor, Jesus, stood in the same spot and talked with a Samaritan woman.

But before we explore that story, let's take in the view. This well stands in a valley between two large mountains. The mountain to our north is Mount Ebal, and the one to the south is Mount Gerizim. The valley stretches west toward the Mediterranean, and were we to drive down this valley, we would come to the ancient city of Samaria just a few miles away.

Take a moment to look at the two mountains. Mount

Ebal, the one to our north, appears to be rather barren, while trees cover a good portion of Mount Gerizim. This can actually help us remember the mountains. Mount Ebal is *bald* while Mount Gerizim is not.

Between the two peaks, nestled nearby in this valley, is the site of the ancient city of Shechem. It's just a little to the west of where we're standing, closer to the base of Mount Ebal. And stretching out behind Shechem is the modern city of Nablus. North of Shechem, clinging to the side of Mount Ebal, is the modern village of Askar, which

Looking up toward Mount Gerizim from near Shechem and Jacob's well

preserves its biblical name, Sychar.

This geographical area appears many times in the Bible. Jacob stopped at Shechem when he returned to the Promised Land. And at the time of the conquest, Joshua gathered all Israel here to recite the blessings and cursings of the covenant. He divided all the people into two groups—one standing on Mount Gerizim and the other on Mount Ebal. The people on Mount Gerizim responded as the blessings of the covenant were read, and the people on Mount Ebal responded as the cursings were read. And, by the way, that can also help us remember the names of the mountains. Cursings are bad, so the mountain associated with the cursings, Mount Ebal, is *evil*. I know—it's a bit corny—but remembering evil, bald Ebal will help you keep your mountains straight!

But let's walk back to Jacob's well, and to the scene in John 4. That Jesus is in Samaria is itself amazing. The Jews and Samaritans had a tumultuous relationship. Each group claimed to be the true followers of God, worshiping in rival temples. About a century and a half before Jesus, the Samaritan temple on Mount Gerizim was destroyed by the leader of Judea, a man named John Hyrcanus. The Samaritans never forgot this event and harbored great hatred for the Jews as a result.

And pious Jews considered the Samaritans to be a racially mixed group who perverted God's Word by setting up this rival worship center. These Jews would cross the Jordan River and walk along the eastern side of the Jordan when traveling between Galilee and Jerusalem to avoid even setting foot in the land of the Samaritans. They preferred to add an extra day to their journey rather than associate with Samaritans.

As John 4 begins, Jesus is traveling from Jerusalem to Galilee. John tells us that Jesus "had to pass through Samaria" (4:4). Was the decision to travel north through Samaria dictated by some pressing appointment in Galilee, or was it required to fulfill the divine appointment that follows in this chapter? I believe that in adding this phrase John is telling us Jesus was compelled to take this route to meet this woman at the well.

John also adds a few other details about this encounter at the well. He says it took place at "the sixth hour" (4:6), which is noon—the hottest part of the day. Jesus sits by the well to rest as the disciples enter the nearby town to buy food. That's when this Samaritan woman comes to the well to draw water. She was from the village of Sychar, a half-mile away. The middle of the day is *not* the best time to take a long walk carrying a heavy clay jar, but this woman didn't want to visit the well when others might be present. She is, as some might euphemistically say today, a "loose woman," and she wants to avoid contact with those who disapprove of her life choices.

Jesus shocks the woman when He speaks to her and requests a drink of water. And His next statement moves her from shock to curiosity. No doubt tired from the endless drudgery of carrying heavy pots of water in the heat of the day, she is intrigued when He offers her a limitless supply of "living water."

The conversation takes an uncomfortable turn for the woman when Jesus tells her to get her husband and return if she wants to know more about this living water. Perhaps her face flushes as Jesus speaks, while her sense of guilt makes her wonder how much this stranger might know. She decides to give a truthful, but deceptive, answer. "I have no husband" (v. 17). But if she hoped her answer would satisfy—and silence—this stranger, she is mistaken.

Jesus reveals His complete knowledge of everything she is trying to conceal. "You have correctly said, 'I have no husband'; for you have had five husbands, and the one whom you now have is not your husband; this you have said truly" (vv. 17–18). This stranger seems to know the most intimate details of her life. But how? No one else from the village had been here to talk with Him. This was more than just a mere man.

The woman speaks her thoughts aloud. "Sir, I perceive that You are a prophet" (v. 19). This man has special insight that can only come from God. And since God knows everything, this man may indeed know her deepest, darkest secrets. And that's when she thinks of a way to turn the spotlight off herself and perhaps even to disengage from this uncomfortable conversation. She decides to throw down the trump card that is sure to bring the discussion to an abrupt end.

"Our fathers worshiped in this mountain," she says, very likely lifting her arm and pointing toward the summit of Mount Gerizim, "and you people say that in Jerusalem is the place where men ought to worship" (John 4:20). This is the heart of the debate, the bone of contention that ultimately divides the Jews and the Samaritans. If she can just get Jesus to begin debating religion, it would move the conversation away from His focus on her relationships and lifestyle choices.

Jesus' response is direct and to the point. He doesn't sidestep her question, the way she has tried to sidestep His. When it comes to form, the Jews indeed have it right, Jesus says. "You worship what you do not know; we worship what we know, for salvation is from the Jews" (John 4:22). God's revelation, His Word, clearly identified the temple in Jerusalem as the place He chose for His glory to dwell.

But having answered her question, Jesus goes beyond it to focus on an even greater truth. The ultimate issue was not *where* one worshiped God but *how* one was to worship God. "But an hour is coming, and now is, when the true worshipers shall worship the Father in spirit and truth; for such people the Father seeks to be His worshipers. God is spirit, and those who worship Him must worship in spirit and truth" (John 4:23–24).

THE REAL ISSUE WHEN IT COMES to worshiping God is not *where* but *how*. It's function over form; substance over style. God is seeking worshipers who worship Him in spirit and in truth. That is, their worship aligns with God's nature and with His character. God is more concerned with the attitude of a person's heart than with the physical location of the place he or she chooses to meet.

Jesus' answer disarms all the defenses this woman tries to construct. All she can finally do is admit that when the Messiah comes "He will declare all things to us" (John 4:25). And Jesus now responds with absolute clarity. "I who speak to you am He" (v. 26). The clearest statement ever made by Jesus that He is the Messiah is spoken to an adulterous woman from a despised race of people—but someone who was willing to listen, and accept, and believe what He had to say.

No large crowd. No beautiful building. No majestic choir or even a praise band. Jesus' greatest message on the essence of worship is delivered to a congregation of one, a woman who is looked down on even by her own people.

As we leave Jacob's well, let's remember the truth the Messiah gives us as well: True worship centers on Jesus, not on us. It's ascribing worth to God, and aligning our lives around Him. The key is not *where* we worship, or *how* we worship, but *who* we worship!

DAY 8

Atop Mount Arbel

For those who've never been to Israel, Mount Arbel is nothing more than an easily forgotten name. It's never mentioned in the Bible, so there's no historical peg on which to hang this geographical spot.

But for those who've hiked to the summit of Mount Arbel, the spot is simply unforgettable. The rubbery legs and burning lungs that make many wonder why they're following their guide to the top of the hill are forgotten as soon as they reach the summit. For many visitors to Israel, Mount Arbel is the first in a string of "Oh, wow!" moments that define their pilgrimage to the land.

What is it about this spot that causes such a reaction—and that stays with these visitors for the rest of their lives? Simply put, it's the view. Mount Arbel is a cliff on the west side of the Sea of Galilee. It rises up in a relatively gentle slope from the west that ends abruptly in a sheer cliff on its northeastern side, right next to the sea. Those walking up the pathway from the west only see the gradual uphill climb until they reach the top. That's when the breathtaking view takes them by surprise. And what a view!

A thousand feet below is the Sea of Galilee. The panoramic view from the top of Mount Arbel allows visitors to see almost the entire lake. And all their misconceptions suddenly vanish. In our mind's eye, when we read about the *Sea* of Galilee, we picture a vast body of water. Certainly that describes the seas we know, like the Atlantic and Pacific Oceans. And the many miracles of Jesus that occurred on the sea—and around its shores—conjure up images of a great body of water where the Son of God demonstrated His power in both word and deed.

But when standing on the summit of Arbel, we look down at a relatively small lake, seven-and-a-half miles wide at its widest point and thirteen miles long. And as we trace the towns along its shore, an even more amazing truth becomes apparent. Most of Jesus' recorded messages and miracles at the Sea of Galilee took place in a very small slice of land along its northern shore.

Capernaum and Bethsaida, two of the three towns where Matthew said Jesus performed most of His mira-

Mount Arbel with the Sea of Galilee in the background

cles, bracket the northern tip of the lake. The third town named by Matthew, Chorazin, sits a little farther north, just up the hillside from the lake. Even if one includes the Mount of Beatitudes, Tabgha (the spot where Jesus likely called His disciples to follow Him), and Kursi (the site where Jesus cast the demons into the herd of swine), the area is still quite small. Much of Jesus' profound ministry took place on a small slice of a tiny lake in an obscure part of an out-of-the-way province in the Roman Empire.

And perhaps that's the most amazing truth we'll carry with us from the summit of Mount Arbel. It's the historical peg that combines with the breathtaking view to make this an unforgettable spot visually and spiritually.

Of all the places God could have chosen to reveal the power and majesty of His Son, He chose "Galilee of the Gentiles" as the prophet described it in Isaiah 9:1–2. "But there will be no more gloom for her who was in anguish; in earlier times He treated the land of Zebulun and the land of Naphtali with contempt, but later on He shall make it glorious, by the way of the sea, on the other side of Jordan, Galilee of the Gentiles. The people who walk in darkness will see a great light; those who live in a dark land, the light will shine on them."

And lest we miss this important truth about Jesus, Matthew reminds us of it as he describes Jesus' ministry. "Now when Jesus heard that John had been taken into custody, He withdrew into Galilee; and leaving Nazareth, He came and settled in Capernaum, which is by the sea, in the region of Zebulun and Naphtali" (Matthew 4:12–13).

Zebulun and Naphtali were two tribal regions near the Sea of Galilee. Even in Isaiah's day, the two regions had been humbled by the surrounding nations, regions Isaiah described as one experiencing gloom, distress, and darkness. In Isaiah 9, God promised to honor this area, the lowest of the low, with the brightness of His light. And according to Matthew 4:14, the reason Jesus centered His ministry around this tiny body of water was to "fulfill what was spoken through Isaiah the prophet."

DON'T MISS THE SIGNIFICANCE

of this connection. Both Isaiah and Matthew remind us that God delights in using the small, the insignificant, the despised, and the neglected to accomplish His great plan. In a day when we assume bigger is better, and equate size with significance, the summit of Mount Arbel is a good spot to remember that God measures importance and success with a different yardstick than that used by the world.

While we're here on top of Mount Arbel, find a spot to sit down. Gaze out over the lake, and focus on that narrow strip of land along its northern shore where Jesus spent most of His time. Pause and compare your life to this lake. What is it that makes you feel insignificant? It might be your background, your education, your current occupation, or even past choices you've made. You love God and want to follow Him, but deep inside do you wonder how He could ever use someone as . . . as insignificant as you?

Thomas Chisholm once described himself as little more than an "old shoe." He trusted in Jesus as his personal Savior when he was twenty-seven and later felt called to ministry. But after serving as a pastor for just one year he had to resign because of poor health—physical problems that plagued him for the rest of his life. Eventually he became a life insurance salesman, but his physical limitations hurt his ability to excel there as well.

In spite of his physical and financial struggles, he never doubted God's faithfulness. In fact, at age seventy-five he gave an honest appraisal of his life when he wrote, "My income has not been large at any time due to impaired health in the earlier years which has followed me on until now. However, I must not fail to record here the unfailing faithfulness of a covenant-keeping God and that He has given me many wonderful displays of His providing care."[1]

Thomas Chisholm couldn't serve with the vigor of others, but he discovered that God is able to demonstrate His awesome power in spite of our limitations. Thomas couldn't do much, but he loved writing poetry. And during his life he wrote over 1,200 poems seeking to serve his Lord through this one avenue God had given him. Most of his poems are unknown today, but one has survived to become a beloved reminder of God's faithfulness in spite of our limitations. He wrote:

"Great is Thy faithfulness," O God my Father,
There is no shadow of turning with Thee;
Thou changest not, Thy compassions,
     they fail not;
As Thou hast been Thou forever wilt be.

Look down from Mount Arbel at that tiny slice
of insignificant shoreline along this small lake in
Galilee and realize that God chose it to be the stage
on which some of the greatest events in world history
unfolded. God delights in using places—and
people—the world sees as insignificant to be the
vessels through which He displays His faithfulness.

Why not let Him use you that way today?

NOTE

1. Kenneth W. Osbeck, *101 Hymn Stories* (Grand Rapids: Kregel, 1982), 84.

DAY 9

Show Dogs and Hunting Dogs

Some years ago when I was living in Texas I talked with a friend about an organization's new chief financial officer. My buddy was a native Texan, and his response came right from the Lone Star State—direct, to the point, and colorful. "The man's a show dog!" Seeing my quizzical expression, he added an equally colorful explanation. "He looks good, but he can't hunt!"

That expression—and its meaning—have stuck with me ever since. We all come across "show dogs" in our lives—men and women who appear competent, sophisticated, distinguished, intelligent, or successful but who can't get the job done. They look good, but they can't hunt!

Jesus had little patience for the show dogs of His day— the hypocritical religious leaders who put on a facade of godliness but didn't know God. And He was equally colorful in His description of these charlatans. "Woe to you, scribes and Pharisees, hypocrites! For you are like whitewashed tombs which on the outside appear beautiful, but inside they are full of dead men's bones and all uncleanness. So you, too, outwardly appear righteous to men, but inwardly you are full of hypocrisy and lawlessness" (Matthew 23:27–28).

From the very beginning of His public ministry, Jesus challenged the show-dog mentality of His day. In the early chapters of the book bearing his name, Matthew paints a picture of Jesus as the ideal Israelite. Just as the nation had its baptismal experience in the Red Sea, Jesus was baptized in the Jordan River. And as Israel went to Mount Sinai to receive the Law, Jesus "went up on the mountain" (Matthew 5:1) and explained the true message of God's Law—and how it ought to be lived out in our lives. We often call this message the Sermon on the Mount, and it's found in Matthew 5–7.

The Bible doesn't tell us the exact location where Jesus delivered the Sermon on the Mount, but the traditional spot overlooking the Sea of Galilee fits the few biblical details recorded. Matthew tells us Jesus was "going throughout Galilee . . . proclaiming the gospel of the kingdom" (Matthew 4:23) when He went up on the mountainside to deliver His message. And when He came "down from the

The chapel on the Mount of Beatitudes

mountain" in Matthew 8:1, the first town He entered was Capernaum. Standing at the entrance to Capernaum today, the dome of the church on the traditional Mount of Beatitudes is visible on top of a hill just a mile to the west.

From the balcony of that church there is a magnificent view of the Sea of Galilee. Grassy fields, interspersed between banana groves, descend toward the water's edge. It's easy to visualize thousands of curiosity seekers flocking to this hillside—or one nearby—to listen to the latest message from this rabbi and perhaps to be an eyewitness to one of His miracles. But whatever brought them to the site, they weren't prepared for the penetrating message He was about to deliver.

Most of us know the beginning of Jesus' message, the Beatitudes, but I want to focus on the rest of the message. Jesus made it clear He had not arrived to do away with God's standards for right and wrong. "Do not think that I came to abolish the Law or the Prophets," He cried. "I did not come to abolish but to fulfill" (Matthew 5:17). He explained the true intent of God's Law, giving several examples. "You have heard that it was said," He announced, giving the standard Pharisaic interpretation of God's Law concerning murder, adultery, divorce, the taking of an oath, seeking revenge, and loving one's neighbor (Matthew 5:21, 27, 31, 33, 38, 43). But He followed each section by explaining God's true intent for that Law with a dramatic contrast: "But I say to you." The difference was profound—like the difference between a show dog and one that can actually hunt.

So what was the standard for obedience that God expected? Jesus gave a summary at the end of Matthew 5. "Therefore you are to be perfect, as your heavenly Father is perfect" (5:48). God's standard is perfection. Jesus achieved that standard. But the religious leaders of His day did not. And if we are honest with ourselves, we need to admit we don't reach that standard either.

Jesus then looked beyond a person's actions to focus on his or her motives. "Beware of practicing your righteousness before men to be noticed by them" (Matthew 6:1). He highlighted the key ways one demonstrated devotion to God in His day—giving to the needy, praying, and fasting. In each case He said a religious hypocrite does the right thing—but for the wrong motives: to be honored by others, to be seen by others, to demonstrate to others his or her devotion to God. Those seeking to impress others forfeit the reward they could have received from God. Jesus' point is profound. If we are really seeking to please God by our actions, then it shouldn't matter whether others even know what we have done.

Jesus ended His message with a series of stern warnings. The way leading to destruction is wide, but the way is narrow that leads to life, and there are few who find it" (Matthew 7:14). "Not everyone who says to Me, 'Lord, Lord,' will enter the kingdom of heaven" (v. 21). He ended His message by comparing those who listen to His words and put them into practice to a wise man who built his house on the rock. In short, obedience to His words would provide stability and serve as a solid foundation to help one withstand life's storms.

And that brings us back to the Sea of Galilee, to Jesus, and to you. Jesus understood the power of storms. He would soon calm a storm on the Sea of Galilee with the simple command, "Peace, be still." More importantly, He understood the sinfulness of the human heart. The religious leaders in Jesus' day sought to meet God's righteous standards by reinterpreting them to make them easier to keep. Don't get me wrong; they still wanted to have standards that were too difficult for most people—but not for themselves. They weren't perfect, but if God would just grade on a curve they would be able to score better than everyone else.

But Jesus knew that dog wouldn't hunt. "For I say to you," He warned, "that unless your righteousness surpasses that of the scribes and Pharisees, you will not enter the kingdom of heaven" (Matthew 5:20). God doesn't grade on a curve, and the only passing grade is 100 percent.

SO WHERE DOES THAT LEAVE US?

The Bible makes it clear that "all have sinned and fall short of the glory of God" (Romans 3:23). No one, no matter how religious, has met God's standard. So can anyone get to heaven? The answer, thankfully, is yes. We can't make it there through our own good works, because none of us can achieve the standard set by God. But Jesus was perfect. He *did* reach that standard. He was the only person who ever lived who could make it to heaven through His own good works. But instead of going straight to heaven, He took a detour that led Him from this hill overlooking the Sea of Galilee to another hill called Golgotha just outside the city of Jerusalem. When Jesus hung on the cross, He did so to pay the penalty for your sin and mine. As the prophet Isaiah predicted seven centuries before the time of Jesus, "But He was pierced through for our transgressions, He was crushed for our iniquities; the chastening for our well-being fell upon Him, and by His scourging we are healed. All of us like sheep have gone astray, each of us has turned to his own way; but the Lord has caused the iniquity of us all to fall on Him" (Isaiah 53:5–6).

So how do we get to heaven? It's not through our own efforts. Rather, we can receive eternal life as a gift by placing our faith and trust in Jesus Christ, and in His death on our behalf. "He made Him who knew no sin to be sin on our behalf, so that we might become the righteousness of God in Him" (2 Corinthians 5:21).

Find a quiet spot and read, slowly and carefully, Matthew 5–7. Note the impossibly high standards required to be righteous before God. Then pause and thank God that Jesus met those standards and willingly went to the cross in your place to pay the penalty for your disobedience.

DAY
10

Jesus and Chorazin

For most pilgrims visiting Israel, Chorazin is a throw-away stop—a bathroom break between the Mount of Beatitudes and a St. Peter's fish lunch at a Jewish kibbutz on the Sea of Galilee. The town was built from basalt stone—a dark, volcanic rock that covers the area around the northern edge of the Sea of Galilee. The restored buildings blend into the surrounding hillside so well that the site is nearly invisible until you are almost upon it.

But once the tourist steps from the bus he or she understands why the noted scholar Jerome Murphy-O'Connor referred to the site as "Capernaum with a view." Nestled up the hillside, away from the shoreline, Chorazin offers a delightful view of the Sea of Galilee. Its ancient inhabitants must also have appreciated the higher elevation, which offered slightly cooler temperatures and less humidity than the villages right along the shore.

But why stop at Chorazin today? The ruins of the ancient synagogue are instructive, but the one at Capernaum is more impressive. A seat of Moses—the place where the rabbi would sit and expound on God's Word—was discovered at Chorazin. But the one inside the synagogue entrance today, while intriguing, is just a copy. The original sits in the Israel Museum in Jerusalem. Tourists enjoy watching for rock badgers—or "coneys" as

Partial ruins of the synagogue in Chorazin

they are called in the King James Version—scampering among the rocks. But is the stop really worth the time it takes? I'm convinced it is, but for a very unusual reason.

If someone asked you to name the three most important cities associated with Jesus, what cities would come to mind? *Bethlehem* . . . the city where He was born, the event heralded by angels and punctuated with a visit from foreign dignitaries bearing expensive gifts? *Nazareth* . . . His boyhood home where an angel announced His miraculous birth to Mary? *Jerusalem* . . . the city of many miracles and of His death and resurrection? Or perhaps *Bethany* . . . the city where He raised Lazarus from the dead and spent so much time with Mary and Martha? None of those four cities made the list compiled by the apostle Matthew. But Chorazin did!

Matthew, the tax collector from Capernaum who became a disciple of Jesus and who wrote the first book of the New Testament, singled out three cities that experienced more miracles of Jesus than any others. And Chorazin is on his list! It, along with Bethsaida and Capernaum, was one of the cities where "most of [Jesus'] miracles were done" (Matthew 11:20).

Impressed? Well, in one sense it does make the site more interesting for visitors. This is *not* a throwaway stop—it is one place where Jesus definitely devoted time and performed many miracles during His ministry in

Galilee. But before you get too excited, name one of the many miracles Jesus performed in this city. If you cannot, don't let it bother you. The Bible doesn't record *any* of the miracles Jesus performed at Chorazin. Had Matthew or Luke not recorded this one statement Jesus made about the town, we would know nothing about His ministry there.

And maybe that's the most important lesson we can carry with us from our brief stop at this site. The Bible is not an exhaustive record of everything Jesus ever said or did. Rather it's a *selective* record of the words and deeds of Jesus that God recorded for our benefit. In describing this in his Gospel account, the apostle John made this fact very clear. "Therefore many other signs Jesus also performed in the presence of the disciples, which are not written in this book; but these have been written so that you may believe that Jesus is the Christ, the Son of God; and that believing you may have life in His name" (John 20:30–31). One chapter later he reaffirmed the fact that his account is only a partial record of all Jesus did. "And there are also many other things which Jesus did, which if they were written in detail, I suppose that even the world itself would not contain the books that would be written" (21:25).

SO WHAT DOES THIS TELL US?

It tells us the Gospel writers were selective in what they recorded about Jesus. Their selectivity was *not* done to edit out or omit items that might have presented Jesus in a lesser light. They weren't trying to hide anything. They make it quite clear that their selective was due to space limitations. A book covering every detail of what Jesus had said and done would have been too massive—too cumbersome— to have been of any practical use to His followers. Under God's sovereign direction the writers of the four Gospels recorded the specific miracles and teachings necessary to preserve accurately the life, ministry, and truth claims of Jesus for later generations.

Chorazin is a city where Jesus performed many miracles, but none of those miracles were essential for our understanding of His person and work . . . and so they were not recorded.

So here's Chorazin today. Fertile ground. An excellent location. But no people. The site is abandoned—as are the other two towns, Bethsaida and Capernaum, where Matthew said Jesus performed most of His miracles. The synagogue is in ruins. Maybe there is one more lesson we need to carry along with us as we leave. These three cities shared one thing in common. They all saw—up close and personal—Jesus' miraculous power. Yet they refused to turn from their sin and acknowledge Him as their Savior.

But what about you? We have a record of many—though not all—of Jesus' miracles and messages. And the apostle John said the record we have was given so that we might believe that Jesus is the Christ—the Messiah—and the Son of God, and that by believing we might have eternal life. Do you believe? If you have not done so before, why not put your trust in Him today as your Savior and Lord?

Stilling the Storm

O f all the trips to Israel I've taken, some of the most rewarding have been the trips with small groups of pastors. It's an opportunity for me to minister to a group of shepherds who spend their lives serving others. And it's fun to watch them relax and allow God's Word to refresh them anew as they experience the places where the events of the Bible actually happened.

When you get a group of pastors off by themselves, out of the spotlight of public ministry, in blue jeans and sneakers, they're a *fun* bunch! Don't get me wrong; they're very serious about the trip, using the time for personal renewal and to help make them better teachers of God's Word. But they're also able to let their guard down, and just be themselves, as they share the experience with a group of their peers.

I remember one vivid moment on such a trip during a blustery January day on the Sea of Galilee. We were beginning the day with a boat ride on the sea. But as we walked down to the dock, the sky didn't look promising. It had rained off and on throughout the night, and the sky was now a dark gray, with low clouds scudding across the mountains on the other side of the lake. A slight breeze was already beginning to roil the water, and the boat was bobbing and bumping against the dock as we walked down to board.

I talked with the captain and he said there was a chance that a sudden storm could come up while we were out on the boat. As a result, he needed to change our planned destination. Rather than sailing from Tiberias out into the middle of the lake and then northwest to Nof Ginosar, he wanted us to sail north, closer to shore, and then return to Tiberias. Flexibility and adaptability are two key components of any trip to Israel, and the captain knew these waters best . . . so we agreed to change our itinerary.

The first part of the trip went well. We made it out to the spot where he thought we would be sheltered from the wind, and then he cut the engine. We gathered the pastors together and started talking about the miracles of Jesus connected with the Sea of Galilee. But about five minutes into our devotional time together a blast of wind hit the boat, causing it to rock from side to side. Though the wind had been blowing from the west, it suddenly seemed to whip around to the southwest, blocking our way back to Tiberias. The captain turned the rudder to try to get the boat to face into the wind, but with every second the wind seemed to grow stronger—and the waves higher. Finally, in the middle of our message the captain gave up and turned on the engine. We might have wanted to preach and pray, but he wanted to get his ship back to land! Now!

For the first time in all my visits to Israel I saw how suddenly, and violently, a storm could break out on the Sea of Galilee. And as we sailed back toward Tiberias, we headed directly into the storm. It was now raining, but the rain wasn't the problem. Instead the ship pitched and tossed as wind-whipped waves crashed over the bow.

And where were the pastors? They were all in the front of the boat, being pelted by the rain and drenched by the breaking waves. And one by one they shouted into the teeth of the storm, "Peace! Be still!" And it quickly became clear they weren't Jesus!

That scene comes back to mind every time I read Mark 4. Actually, to understand the events of Mark 4 we need to look at both that chapter as well as Matthew 8. Taken together, they describe one of the busiest days in the life of Jesus. In Matthew 8:5–16, we read a grocery list of miracles performed by Jesus, one after another, in Capernaum. Jesus healed the centurion's servant and Peter's mother-in-law along with "many who were demon-possessed" and "all who were ill" (v. 16). It must have been a patient-packed day for the Great Physician.

But it seems that miracles weren't the only thing Jesus did on that day. Mark 4 tells us Jesus "began to teach again by the sea" that same day. The crowds became so large that "He got into a boat in the sea and sat down; and the

A boat ride on the Sea of Galilee

whole crowd was by the sea on the land" (4:1). Jesus then taught the multitudes. It was a day booked solid with ministering to the spiritual and physical needs of the people.

And as the day ended Jesus gave His disciples instructions to "go over to the other side" of the lake (v. 35). Mark records that they left the crowd behind and "took Him along with them in the boat, just as He was" (v. 36), probably meaning that they began rowing away as soon as He finished teaching, rather than first heading back to shore.

We often misunderstand what happened next. Some translations say "a furious squall came up" or "a huge storm came up," and we picture a massive thunderstorm, with driving rain and jagged bolts of lightning, followed by the clap of thunder. But Mark, who based his Gospel on the eyewitness testimony of Peter, provides a far more accurate description. He writes that the boat encountered a "fierce gale of wind" (v. 37). While this storm might have been accompanied by rain and lightning, that's *not* what frightened the disciples. They focused instead on the waves that were "breaking over the boat so much that the boat was already filling up" with water (v. 37).

And where was Jesus when all this was taking place? As the water poured over the side near the front of the boat, He was "in the stern, asleep on the cushion" (v. 38). After an exhausting day of ministry, the rocking of the boat had lulled Him into a deep, sound sleep. In their fear the disciples "woke him" and shouted, "Teacher, do You not care that we are perishing?"

And Jesus responded by showing He was much more than just a mere human. He got up and "rebuked the wind, and said to the sea, 'Hush, be still!' And the wind died down and it became perfectly calm" (v.39). The old King James expression "Peace. Be still" has a holy aura about it. But if I can offer a more literal translation of what Jesus said, it would be "Quiet! Settle down!"

And with those words the power of the divine Son of God exploded onto this scene. The wind stopped, and the sea became calm. The verb tenses used imply that both actions happened immediately. The wind didn't gradually die down and the waves didn't get progressively smaller. They stopped!

And the disciples, who had been afraid of the storm, now became terrified as they stared at Jesus. "Who then is this," they asked, "that even the wind and the sea obey Him?" (v. 41). We know the answer. Jesus is the divine Son of God who made the heavens and the earth. And as Creator He has the power to control all He has made.

HERE ARE TWO LESSONS FOR US

from Jesus' windy encounter on the Sea of Galilee. First, in seeing Jesus become so exhausted that He could sleep through a fierce storm, we're reminded of His humanity. Jesus understands the pressures and problems we face as humans. He was tired that evening. The writer of Hebrews says that on earth Jesus shared in our humanity so He could become our "merciful and faithful high priest" (Hebrews 2:17).

The second lesson comes from Jesus' response to the storm once He was awakened. He speaks, and the waves stop. As the divine Son of God He has the power to change life's circumstances and to calm life's storms.

So what are the problems that seem to be crashing down on you today? Isn't it comforting to know Jesus understands . . . and that He has the ability to stand beside you and to say to life's storms, "Hush! Settle down!" Just like the disciples, call out to Him for help, and then watch what He will do!

DAY
12

The Deviled Ham Man from Horse Town

Want a quick test to see how old you are? It's very simple. I'll say two words, and you tell me what comes to mind. Here they are: "flannel board."

If nothing comes to mind, it's likely you grew up in the VHS/DVD/Blu-ray generations—the generations that learned Bible lessons by watching a VeggieTales video or some other modern media production. But for the rest of you—and here I'm speaking largely to the members of the AARP generation!—the words "flannel board" conjure up images from childhood days in Sunday school. Bible stories told by teachers slapping cutout characters on a cloth-covered board resting on an easel.

Those flannel-board visuals, as quaint and outdated as they now seem, helped bring the Bible to life for a generation of children. And I happen to be one of them! One of the most memorable stories to me was the account of Jesus casting demons out of a man and into a herd of swine. I can still see the teacher reaching up to position the pigs, having them tumble off the cliff into the Sea of Galilee below. We went home picturing those pigs doing their "swine dive" into the water.

Unfortunately, once I finally got to Israel I discovered there is *no* cliff anywhere on the eastern side of the Sea of Galilee, which is where the story took place. But seeing the spot where the events happened was even more dramatic than the flannelgraph version. In fact, let's visit the site today.

Watch your step as you get down from the bus. We're just going to walk up this path for about thirty feet. But do me a favor and stay *on* the sidewalk. See that small yellow sign with a red triangle hanging from the fence? That means there's a minefield just on the other side of the fence. From 1948 until 1967 the spot where we're standing was the border between Israel and Syria. As you can tell from the sign warning about land mines, it wasn't a friendly border!

Ah, here we are! Now look toward the north. See that clump of trees just to the right of the road about a half-mile away? Just behind those trees are the ruins of an ancient Byzantine monastery. Notice how it's not right along the shore. Instead, it's hugging the base of those hills that rise up to become the Golan Heights.

An ancient harbor was once found along the shore in that same general area. That was the harbor for the small town of Gergesa, and it's likely the spot where the boat with Jesus and His disciples landed. So, why was the monastery built outside the town, at the foot of the hills? To answer that question, we need to look carefully at the story in Mark 5. Mark tells us the demon-possessed man came "from the tombs" (5:2) to meet Jesus. "Constantly

Standing on the steep bank leading down to the Sea of Galilee at Kursi/Gergesa

night and day, he was screaming among the tombs and in the mountains, and gashing himself with stones" (v. 5).

People weren't buried inside cities and towns. Instead, the graves were located outside of town . . . but not too far away since people had to carry the body to the burial spot. So where were the tombs for the town of Gergesa? Probably somewhere near the spot where the monastery and the accompanying chapel were built, at the base of the hills.

Now, keep looking toward the monastery. This site is unusual because archaeologists also found a second, smaller chapel nearby, just up the hillside from the monastery itself. Look slightly to the right of a stand of trees and about one hundred yards up the hill. See that area that has been excavated? That's the chapel. But why put another chapel further up the hillside? Possibly it was built to remember the spot where the demon-possessed man lived in the hills.

After confronting the demons that were controlling this poor man, Jesus commanded them to come out of him. So many evil spirits were living inside the man they had named their host "Legion." How many demons were there? We don't know for sure, but the Bible gives us two clues. First, a Roman legion was made up of six thousand men. And second, when the demons left the man they entered a herd of two thousand swine. This man seems to have been the most extreme example of demon possession that Jesus encountered during His earthly ministry.

Mark tells us there was "a large herd of swine feeding nearby on the mountain" (v. 11). Do we know which specific hill? There's one additional detail that can help us identify it. When the demons entered the pigs, they "rushed down the steep bank into the sea" and were drowned (v. 13). So the hillside where the pigs were grazing must have a steep bank that leads all the way down to the water's edge.

Look back to the north. From where we're standing all the way to the northern edge of the lake, there isn't a single spot where the mountains extend down to the edge of the sea. Instead, a relatively flat plain extends all along the water's edge. Now, turn the other way and look south. There's that same flat plain all along the water's edge, all the way to the southern tip of the Sea of Galilee.

Okay, now look at the spot where we're standing. As you turn and look toward the water, see how the hill on which we're standing goes right down to the water's edge. It's not a cliff, but it's fair to call this a "steep bank," don't you think?

If we look behind us at the hill rising up to the east, we can see the notch that has been cut out of the hill for the modern highway. Mentally fill that back in and follow the ridge we're standing on all the way up the mountain. This finger of land is the only ridge that extends from the top of the mountain all the way down, ending with a "steep bank" that leads to the water's edge.

You're standing at the spot where the pigs ran down the mountain!

But there is still one more detail before we leave. After casting out the demons Jesus told the man, in 5:19, to "Go home to your people and report to them what great things the Lord has done for you, and how He had mercy on you." We'd expect the man to go to the town of Gergesa about a half-mile to the north. But instead, the man "went away and began to proclaim in Decapolis what great things Jesus had done for him" (v. 20). But where is Decapolis?

"Decapolis" means "ten cities," and this was a league of cities that shared a common Greek and Roman culture. Most were located along the eastern side of the Jordan Valley. The northernmost city was Hippos, which is the Greek word for "horse." And where is this town? Look again to the south. See that group of houses and trees right along the shore, about a half-mile away? Just to the east of that spot is the hill on which Hippos stood. You can't see it from here, but it will come into view in less than a minute once we start driving.

That must be the man's hometown. That's where he went to share the good news about Jesus. The deviled ham man from the horse town went back changed—"clothed and in his right mind"—at peace with himself and with God (v. 15).

OKAY, BACK ON THE BUS! BUT AS
we get ready to drive away I want to ask you an important question. What lesson can we learn from this story about the deviled ham man from the horse town?

I believe the key lesson is the trustworthiness of the Bible. Even when it comes to small details—like tombs among the hills, or a steep bank leading into the sea, or a town of the Decapolis that must be nearby—the writers were careful historians. The entire account has the ring of authenticity, even down to the tiniest details. But why was it important to get the details right?

Peter, the apostle who was the eyewitness source behind Mark's Gospel, says it this way in 2 Peter 1:16. "For we did not follow cleverly devised tales when we made known to you the power and coming of our Lord Jesus Christ, but we were eyewitnesses of His majesty." Truthfulness and reliability. That's why it was so important for the writers to get even the tiniest details right.

Sometime today pull out your Bible and hold it in your hand. Then say to yourself, "I can trust this book!" That's the lesson you can take away from the story about the "deviled ham man from horse town."

DAY 13

The Two-Part Miracle

Ever have an off day? You know, one of those days when you're just not running on all cylinders. You wake up late because you forgot to set your alarm. You run to the bathroom, hit the light switch, and see a momentary flash as the bulb in the ceiling light burns out. You pour yourself a bowl of cereal and take your first bite only to discover the milk has soured. You run out the door and realize it's raining—and you left your umbrella at the office.

My dad loves baseball, and his expression for those kind of days comes right from the ballpark. "You're in a slump."

We all have times when we seem to be in a slump. It's just part of life. But did Jesus ever have an off day? Was there ever a time when He was in a slump? If you've read the account of the miracle recorded in Mark 8, you might think so!

This is one of those stories that, at first, seems very confusing. It begins in Bethsaida, on the northeast side of the Sea of Galilee. "Bethsaida" means "house of fishing," and according to John 1:44 it was the original hometown of Philip, Peter, and Andrew. So it's no surprise that Peter and Andrew were fishermen, or that Jesus spent time in Bethsaida.

The surprise comes when people bring a blind man to Jesus to be healed. After leading the man outside town, Mark records that "after spitting on his eyes and laying His hands on him" Jesus asked the man, "Do you see anything?" (Mark 8:23). The man answered, "I see men, for I see them like trees, walking around" (v. 24).

And that's where many have a problem with this story! At first, it looks like Jesus was having an off day. He tried to heal the man, but the miracle came up just a little short. Jesus had to put His hands on the man's eyes a second time before the man could finally see everything clearly. So is this a case where Jesus had to redo the miracle to get it right?

Everything else we know about Jesus tells us clearly that the answer is no. Jesus didn't have an off day. Nor did He have to redo a miracle before He could get it right.

Mark is the only one of the four Gospels that records this miracle, so to understand what's happening we need to look more closely at this small book.

Some think of the Gospel of Mark as the *Reader's Digest* condensed version of the Gospels. That is, they see it as little more than a synopsis of Matthew and Luke. Don't have enough time to read the longer Gospel accounts? Then just read Mark. In this view, Mark is the *Cliffs Notes* Gospel—the abridged summary containing just the high

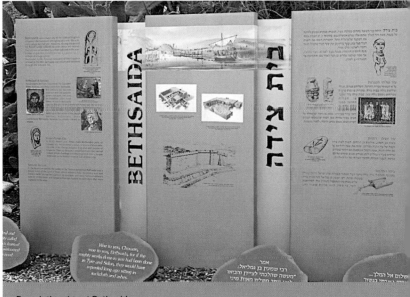

Descriptive sign at Bethsaida

points and key events from the other accounts.

Such a view couldn't be further from the truth, and this miracle is one key example. If Mark is nothing more than a summary of the other Gospels, then why does Mark include a miracle that isn't in any of the other accounts?

Mark had a distinct purpose in writing his Gospel, and this miracle plays a pivotal role in his tracing of the life of Christ. Under the guidance of the Holy Spirit, Mark set out to write an account of the life of Jesus for a Roman audience. In his first sentence he set out the purpose for his work. It is "the gospel of Jesus Christ, the Son of God." He was writing to share the gospel, that is the good news, about Jesus, who was the Messiah (the Christ) *and* the Son of God.

Direct. To the point. And concise. That characterizes the entire Gospel of Mark. And to drive home his message, Mark includes two major miracles of sight followed by two major confessions. The first of the miracles of restoring sight to the blind is this one, and it's followed immediately by Peter's confession. When Jesus asked, "Who do you say that I am?" Peter's response was, "You are the Christ" (Mark 8:29).

Peter had spiritual insight, but it was not fully developed. He got the first part of the message right—Jesus was the Messiah. But he didn't fully comprehend the rest of the truth—Jesus was also the Son of God who "must suffer many things and be rejected by the elders and the chief priests and the scribes, and be killed, and after three days rise again" (v. 31). Peter only had partial sight into the real identity and ministry of Jesus, which is shown by his attempt to rebuke Jesus for predicting His coming death (v. 32).

Mark follows this miracle of sight and confession with Jesus' teaching on discipleship that climaxes in His announcement in Mark 10:45. "For even the Son of Man did not come to be served, but to serve, and to give His life a ransom for many." Peter—and the rest of the disciples—needed additional insight into the person and work of Jesus before they could fully comprehend who He was . . . and what He expected of them as His disciples.

After focusing on Jesus' teaching regarding discipleship, Mark presents his second miracle of restoring sight to the blind—the healing of Bartimaeus in Mark 10. No two-stage process here. Bartimaeus is healed instantly because of His faith. And as a good disciple, he immediately began "following Him on the road" (v. 52; for details of this marvelous miracle read pages 177–82). This second miracle of healing will be followed by the second confession, this time by a Roman centurion. It takes place just as Jesus dies on the cross, with the curtain of the temple being torn in two from top to bottom. The Roman centurion overseeing the crucifixion responds to these events by crying out, "Truly this man was the Son of God!" (Mark 15:39).

Mark's message is the good news that Jesus is the Messiah—and that He is the Son of God. The disciples, represented by Peter, get it partly right early on. He is the Messiah. But they still don't see clearly. It's not till the end of the book that someone—and he happens to be a Roman!—sees the rest of the picture. Jesus is *also* the Son of God who dies to pay the divine debt for the sins of the world.

So, why a partial miracle in Mark 8? Mark records this miracle because it illustrates the partial under-standing of the disciples. The miracle speaks to their lack of spiritual insight, not to any inability on the part of Jesus. The man who saw people like trees was a visual picture of the followers of Jesus who themselves had only partial insight into His person and work. They could see He was the Messiah, but they didn't yet understand He was the Son of God who had come to die for the sins of the world, nor did they fully realize what it meant to be one of His disciples.

Moments after the partial healing, Jesus placed His hands on the man's eyes and his vision "was restored, and [he] began to see everything clearly" (v. 25). Having used the blind man's gaining of partial sight as an object lesson, Jesus then healed him fully.

But let's return to Bethsaida one last time. The Gospel of Matthew tells us this was one of the towns in which most of Jesus' miracles were done, but Mark 8 records the only known miracle connected with Bethsaida. And in this account Jesus led the man *outside* the town before performing the miracle. And once the man was healed, Jesus sent him home and told him not to go into the village. Why?

Perhaps the reason is that this miracle had nothing to do with the unbelieving people of Bethsaida. Remember, the town is later judged by Jesus because of its unbelief. The miracle wasn't for the benefit of the town. Rather, it was an illustration—an object lesson—for His disciples. They had some insight, but there was still much for them to learn.

AS WE WALK AWAY FROM

Bethsaida, back toward the Sea of Galilee, perhaps that should be the lesson for us as well. If you have placed your trust in Jesus as your Savior, you have some depth of spiritual insight. But you still only have partial sight. There's much for us yet to learn, and Jesus wants to lead us on a path of discipleship that will result in ever-clearer spiritual insight. Partial sight is better than blindness, but 20/20 vision is even better.

Continue on as a disciple of Jesus—and watch your spiritual vision improve!

DAY
14

Caesarea Philippi—
Peter and Pan

W e're standing at Banias, which is really Panias . . . but we know it as Caesarea Philippi. Confused? If you're not, you've either been to Israel, or you're not telling the truth!

Okay, here's the longer version. And to understand it, stand here beside me and look up at Mount Hermon. Actually, we can only see a small part of the mountain from here. We're too close to get a proper sense of its true size. Now look at the spring of water flowing from the base of the mountain. See that large cave just above it? At one point in history the water actually flowed out of the cave itself.

But back to the name. When Alexander the Great came through this area, his conquest brought with it the

Greek language and culture. And this spot, with its flowing stream and lush vegetation, seemed like the perfect place to worship the Greek god Pan, the god of shepherds, flocks, and nature. So the place eventually became known as Panias: "Pan's place."

During the Muslim conquests the invaders brought a new language, Arabic, to the region. And Arabic lacks a *P* sound. The closest sound to it in Arabic is *B*. As a result, Panias became Banias, which is the name it has today.

But if all that's true, why do we call this place Caesarea Philippi? That's where politics comes into play. Herod Philip, one of Herod the Great's sons, gained control of the territory east of the Jordan River, including the area of Panias, after his father's death. He built up the area around Panias and dedicated it to Caesar. But since his father had already built the city of Caesarea out on the coast, Philip named his city Caesarea Philippi—"Philip's city for Caesar." He could change the official name of the city, but he couldn't change the history of the region or the hearts of the people. They kept calling it Panias, and that's the name that stuck long after the buildings of the city fell into disuse.

But during the New Testament era the region was officially know as Caesarea Philippi, and Jesus and His disciples visited here at least once. Imagine what it was like for Jesus and His followers to enter this pagan city. A temple dedicated to Augustus stood directly in front of the cave of Pan, and the life-giving water from the cave seemed to flow out from this monument. Next to it was the court of Pan and the nymphs, and beside that stood the temple to Zeus, the king of the gods.

Certainly this kind of idolatry, right in the very land God had promised to His people, was an affront to any true believer. How could God allow such evil to continue? Little wonder that most pious Jews were looking for a military Messiah, a conquering hero who would purge the

Looking toward the cave at Caesarea Philippi, located at the base of Mount Hermon

land of its pagan overlords and their false gods.

And maybe that's one reason so many people struggled with Jesus. They were looking for a Messiah who would be a sword-wielding soldier, not a humble shepherd. Jesus didn't match their expectations.

Perhaps that's why Jesus took His followers on this field trip to Caesarea Philippi—away from the pious masses and into the very heart of a pagan stronghold. This was the perfect spot to quiz His followers on the key issues of His life and ministry.

Jesus wanted His disciples first to explain who others thought He was. So in Matthew 16:13–14 He asked, "Who do people say that the Son of Man is?" They answered, "Some say John the Baptist; and others, Elijah; but still others, Jeremiah, or one of the prophets." People recognized that Jesus was no ordinary man, and they were even willing to admit that He was a prophet. And the three candidates suggested by the people are significant.

John the Baptist was the most amazing and dramatic prophet raised up by God at the time of Jesus. And in the Old Testament Elijah and Jeremiah were willing to stand alone for God in times of great distress and spiritual darkness.

The people were willing to concede Jesus was a prophet, but that was as far as they would go. So Jesus then turned the spotlight on His own followers in verse

15. "Who do you say that I am?" And good old Peter gets it right! "You are the Christ, the Son of the living God."

Pay careful attention to Peter's words. Jesus was more than just a prophet. He was also the Christ, the Anointed One—the Messiah. If He didn't match people's perceptions of what the Messiah was to be, it's because their perceptions were flawed. He *is* the promised Messiah.

Just as importantly, Peter declared that Jesus is *the Son of the living God*. This is a remarkable affirmation of both the power of God and the deity of Jesus. The God of Israel is the only *living* God; and Jesus, Israel's Messiah, is God's eternal Son. In verse 17, Jesus commended Peter for his spiritual understanding. "Blessed are you, Simon Barjona, because flesh and blood did not reveal this to you, but My Father who is in heaven."

Think about the conversation that just took place. It might have happened right beside this gurgling stream. Perhaps the birds were chirping and the leaves rustling in the wind, just like most other days. But on that amazingly ordinary day, something extraordinary happened. God the Father opened Peter's heart and mind to enable him to understand a profound spiritual truth. Most were willing to accept Jesus as a prophet, but that was all. Peter recognized Jesus for who He really was.

THE TRUTH REVEALED TO PETER
is still the truth that separates followers of Jesus
today from our Jewish and Muslim friends. Jesus'
question is one each of us must answer today: "Who
do you say that I am?" Is He a good man? Perhaps
even a prophet? He is that, but His words and actions
show He is much more. From His birth in Bethlehem
to His Palm Sunday ride into Jerusalem on a colt, the
foal of a donkey, He fulfilled countless prophecies
that identified Him as Israel's promised Messiah. But
even more than that He showed He is God's eternal
Son, which makes Him Lord of all. And now He wants
to be your personal Savior. That's why He willingly
died on the cross to pay the eternal penalty for your
and my sins. His resurrection from the dead proves
that full payment was made.

If you have not already done so, why not make
Jesus—the Messiah and God's Son—your Savior
today? The apostle Paul described how in his letter to
the church at Rome. "If you confess with your mouth
Jesus as Lord, and believe in your heart that God
raised Him from the dead, you will be saved"
(Romans 10:9). Jesus is the Messiah; He's God's
eternal Son, and He wants to be your Savior!

DAY 15

The Transfiguration

Ask the typical tourist to name his or her favorite spot on a trip to Israel, and the results are fairly predictable. The Sea of Galilee. Capernaum. The Mount of Beatitudes. The Mount of Olives. The Garden of Gethsemane. The Garden Tomb.

Most tourists' "top-ten lists" include these sites, which usually have two things in common. First, most are connected in some way with the life of Jesus. And second, they're not totally obscured by a church or religious shrine. The sites preserve some sense of what it might have looked like when the events of the Bible took place there.

For example, at the far northern edge of Israel, on the Golan Heights, pilgrims come for a panoramic view of

Mount Hermon, which is a likely candidate for the Mount of Transfiguration. Mount Hermon is not the *traditional* site of the Mount of Transfiguration; that honor belongs to Mount Tabor. However, that tradition didn't arise until several centuries after the time of Jesus. Nothing in the biblical account points to Mount Tabor as the actual location.

Caesarea Philippi stood at the base of Mount Hermon. In Matthew and Mark the transfiguration of Jesus is said to have taken place six days after Peter's amazing confession at Caesarea Philippi. Luke says the event happened "about eight days" later. While some see this as an error in the Bible, New Testament commentator John MacArthur doesn't believe it's a contradiction at all. He says Luke merely "bookended the six days" by adding the day Peter made his confession as well as the actual day of the transfiguration.[1] While the time between Peter's confession and the Mount of Transfiguration is sufficient to walk a great distance, each of the three Synoptic Gospels connects the two events.

Luke says the transfiguration took place on a "mountain," but Matthew and Mark both add that it was a "high" mountain. So how high are the mountains in the area? While Mount Tabor rises to a respectable 1,850 feet, Mount Hermon, at over 9,200 feet, towers above every other mountain in Israel. On a clear day Mount Hermon can be seen from the Sea of Galilee, forty miles away.

That's a high mountain!

Imagine being one of the three disciples up on the mountain with Jesus. It sounds exciting, special, like a once-in-a-lifetime opportunity. But that's looking at it after the fact. Frankly, the three disciples were worn out and tired. Luke delicately puts it this way. As the transfiguration began, the three disciples "had been overcome with sleep" (Luke 9:32). I suspect they nodded off and were roused back to consciousness when they somehow realized Jesus was talking with some visitors.

Mount Hermon from the Sea of Galilee

The first thing they noticed as they awakened was the remarkable change in Jesus' appearance. Matthew says His face "shone like the sun" while His clothes "became as white as light" (Matthew 17:1–2). Mark said His clothing became "radiant and exceedingly white, as no launderer on earth can whiten them" (Mark 9:3). Luke said His face changed, and His clothes "became white and gleaming" (Luke 9:29).

The writers are struggling to find illustrations that describe what the disciples saw. Staring at Jesus was like trying to look directly into the sun. He was totally engulfed by a brightness, radiating from within, that was blinding in its brilliance. These disciples caught a glimpse of Jesus in all His heavenly glory, the same glory Jesus later said the world will someday see at His second coming.

Two figures appeared beside Jesus, and they're identified as Moses and Elijah. How did the disciples know who they were? Obviously they weren't wearing name tags saying, "Hello, I'm Moses," or "My name is Elijah." And no paintings or pictures existed of either man. So how did they know who they were? Almost certainly, the disciples knew because Jesus addressed them by name.

Imagine, seeing Jesus in His heavenly splendor . . . and then listening to a conversation between Jesus and arguably the two greatest prophets of the Old Testament. And what did they talk about? We know that Moses and

Elijah "were speaking of His departure which He was about to accomplish at Jerusalem" (Luke 9:31). The focus of the conversation was the coming crucifixion—Jesus' death in Jerusalem to pay for the sins of the world.

And it was at this point that Peter defaulted to his classic response mechanism: Open your mouth and say the first thing that comes to mind. "Lord, it is good for us to be here; if You wish, I will make three tabernacles here, one for You, and one for Moses, and one for Elijah" (Matthew 17:4). Mark and Luke add that Peter said this out of sheer fright because he didn't know what else to say!

Think about this. Moses was the great Old Testament prophet who had announced that the seed of a woman would crush the head of the serpent, though in doing so the serpent would strike at His heel. And Elijah was the prophet whom Malachi said would appear before the "great and terrible day of the LORD" comes on the earth (Malachi 4:5). Both men were now standing in front of the disciples discussing the central prophetic event in all history, an event that was about to take place in Jerusalem.

And Peter responds by suggesting they start a building program!

Why did Peter want to build three booths? Some think it was to provide shelter for the three men now in front of him, perhaps to keep them in place, and maybe to keep the conversation going. But Luke adds a detail that makes this unlikely. He said Peter made the suggestion "as these were leaving Him." Moses and Elijah were already on their way back to heaven when Peter suggested building the booths.

A second possibility is that Peter wanted to build a memorial to commemorate the event that had just taken place. Certainly it's in our human nature to want to build memorials to commemorate historical events. Look at all the shrines and monuments we've built over the years. In fact, I remember Peter's words every time I visit the churches built on top of sacred sites throughout the Holy Land. They are shrines built by well-intentioned people who, like Peter, wanted to memorialize key events in Bible history.

There's a third possibility why Peter wanted to build the three booths. The Feast of Booths, or Feast of Tabernacles, was a feast that looked toward the final regathering of Israel and the inauguration of the kingdom. Zechariah the prophet predicted a time when those "who are left of all the nations that went against Jerusalem will go up from year to year to worship the King, the Lord of hosts, and to celebrate the Feast of Booths" (Zechariah 14:16). Perhaps Peter wanted to build the booths to commemorate this time of glory that he was certain must be coming soon.

But if that's the case, Peter missed the point. He, and all the disciples, kept looking for the kingdom, while Moses and Elijah were talking with Jesus about the cross. God had to interrupt Peter by telling him, "This is My beloved Son, with whom I am well-pleased; listen to Him!" (Matthew 17:5). Peter got so wrapped up in the vision and in his grandiose plans that he missed the content of the message being discussed.

THE BEST LESSON WE CAN TAKE from this amazing experience on Mount Hermon is this: We need to keep our focus on Jesus. Instead of trying to help Him out with our efforts, as Peter hoped to do, let's pay closer attention to what the Bible says about Him—who He is, what He has done, and what He has said He will do in the future. God announced from heaven that Jesus is His beloved Son. Let's pause what we're doing and listen to what He has to say!

NOTE

1. John MacArthur, *Luke 6–10*, The MacArthur New Testament Commentary (Chicago: Moody, 2011), 281–82.

DAY
16

Feeding the Five Thousand

Of all the miracles performed by Jesus, only one is recorded in all four Gospels—the feeding of the five thousand. For that reason alone it's one of the best-known miracles of our Lord. Yet many details of the miracle, including its location, are wrapped in obscurity.

Today a tour guide might take you to a place called Tabgha on the shore of the Sea of Galilee, a beautiful spot about one and one-half miles southwest of Capernaum. There, near the base of the hill that we know today as the Mount of Beatitudes, you can view a mosaic from an early church that pictures five small loaves of bread and two fish. The guide will point to the mosaic and say you're at the traditional spot for the feeding of the five thousand.

This might be a wonderful place to remember that

miracle, but it's *not* the spot where the miracle occurred. To understand why, let's look carefully at the details in the four Gospels.

Matthew provides a good summary of the events surrounding this miracle. In Matthew 13:54, Jesus visited His "hometown" of Nazareth. He was in the region of Galilee, which was ruled at that time by Herod the tetrarch—a son of Herod the Great who was also known as Herod Antipas. As Matthew 14 begins Herod had received reports about the miracles being performed by Jesus, and he was alarmed. He thought perhaps Jesus might be John the Baptist returning from the dead, which was upsetting since he's the one who put John to death! Herod must have responded by sending some of his forces to investigate the reports.

Matthew described Jesus' reaction to Herod's concern. "Now when Jesus heard about John, He withdrew from there in a boat to a secluded place by Himself" (Matthew 14:13). When Jesus heard Herod Antipas was focused on His ministry, He sailed to the other side of the Sea of Galilee. The Jordan River was the boundary of Herod's kingdom. By sailing to the eastern side of the lake, Jesus left Herod's jurisdiction. Matthew then records the miraculous feeding of the five thousand, which took place in "a secluded place" somewhere on that side of the lake.

Briefly, let's consider Jesus' activities after this miracle.

Jesus commanded the disciples to "go ahead of Him to the other side" (Matthew 14:22) while He stayed on the mountain to pray. After that, Jesus caught up with His disciples by walking on the water. But as amazing as that story is, let's jump instead to the end of the account. Matthew concludes by noting that "when they had crossed over, they came to land at Gennesaret" (Matthew 14:34). This is the Greek transliteration of the Hebrew word *Kinneret*, and

The northeastern side of the Sea of Galilee, in the general area of the feeding of the 5,000

the ancient site of Kinneret was just south of Tabgha.

So Jesus started in the region of Herod and crossed over the Sea of Galilee to leave Herod's jurisdiction. The feeding of the five thousand then took place somewhere on the eastern side of the Sea of Galilee. After the miracle the disciples got in the boat and crossed back to the western side of the Sea, eventually landing at Gennesaret, near Tabgha. The feeding of the five thousand couldn't have taken place at Tabgha because it's on the wrong side of the lake.

Matthew recorded one additional detail that's rather important. We refer to this miracle as the feeding of the five thousand, but that's not quite accurate. He reports that "there were about five thousand men who ate, besides women and children" (Matthew 14:21). When the women and children were added in, the total number fed could have easily been ten thousand or more.

Mark also said the miracle took place in a "secluded place" (Mark 6:32), which he later called a "desolate" place (v. 35). However, he also noted there were villages in the surrounding countryside. And Dr. Luke reported that the miracle took place somewhere near Bethsaida (Luke 9:10), though in a "desolate place" (v. 12) rather than at the city itself. Bethsaida is on the northeastern shore of the Sea of Galilee, so Luke helps us narrow down the general location for the miracle.

Some have been confused because Mark 6:45 says that when Jesus dismissed the crowd He "made His disciples get into the boat and go ahead of Him to the other side to Bethsaida." But how could they get in a boat and head *toward* Bethsaida if they were already on the eastern side of the lake near Bethsaida to begin with? At first glance it appears from this verse that Bethsaida is on the opposite side of the lake from where the miracle occurred. But this would seem to contradict all the other Gospel accounts.

The solution to this apparent problem is found by looking at what Mark actually wrote in the original Greek version of the account. In giving directions, Mark used two different Greek prepositions. First, Jesus gave the disciples orders to go "to the other side." Mark used the Greek preposition *eis*, which indicates direction to a place. The destination to which they were heading was "the other side." Then, much like a modern GPS, Jesus clarified the specific *route* they were to take to reach that destination. They were to travel *pros* Bethsaida. That is, they were to go along the northern edge of the lake—by or toward or around Bethsaida—rather than try to take a shortcut directly across the lake. The windstorm that follows indicates Jesus was giving wise advice to stick to the shoreline. Thus Mark 6:45 would suggest the feeding of the five thousand took place further to the east of Bethsaida, on the very northeastern edge of the Sea of Galilee because the disciples had to go past Bethsaida on their journey west.

The apostle John provides one additional detail. He notes that the "Passover, the feast of the Jews, was near" (John 6:4). Passover is in March or April, so the feeding of the five thousand took place in the spring of the year. This is one of the most beautiful times of the year in Israel. The winter rains are just coming to an end and the hillsides are covered in a carpet of green. Mark reported that Jesus had the people sit on the *green* grass (Mark 6:39), confirming the time of the year.

BUT OUR TIME TOGETHER SO FAR today has sounded more like a geography lesson than a devotional. What can we take away from this time with Jesus on the northeastern shore of the Sea of Galilee? I want us to sail away from this spot carrying two key truths.

First, we can trust the Bible. Each Gospel writer tells the story of Jesus from his own unique perspective, but the accounts are not in conflict. Instead, they're more like watching a 3D movie. When viewed together, they help provide depth, dimension, and texture to the ministry of Jesus. Each writer focused on different parts of the whole to present his account. But what they recorded is true, and as a result we can harmonize the accounts.

Second, it's the *person*, not the *place*, that's significant. Frankly, I love the fact that we don't know the specific hill on which the feeding of the five thousand took place. Had it been known, it would long ago have been torn up by some religious group wanting to build a shrine on the site. Don't get me wrong. I'm not against trying to locate the spot where specific events happened. Mark Twain understood the importance of building churches to commemorate events in the Holy Land. He described it in his classic travelogue, *The Innocents Abroad*, as driving "a stake through a pleasant tradition that will hold it to its place forever."

But sometimes the shrine can overshadow the person or event it was built to honor. And the reality of what God did at that place in the past gets lost in all the religious traditions that grow up like weeds all over the site. And that's why I like to look at the hills of the Golan Heights as we drive around the northeastern edge of the Sea of Galilee. It's still remote; it's still covered in grass. It's still just the same as it was when Jesus divided the multitude into companies of fifty and one hundred and fed them with the five loaves and two fish that were the lunch of a small boy. I look at those hills and I can see the miracle taking place. I see the land, and I open the Book. But my ultimate focus is on God and His Son.

And that's what God intended all along!

DAY
17

Feeding the Four Thousand

Let's face it, we like being first. Given a choice, all of us would prefer receiving the blue ribbon or gold medal to being honored as first runner-up. People remember who came in first, but most forget who was second.

They know, for example, that Roger Bannister was the first athlete to run the mile in under four minutes, but who remembers the second runner to do so, John Landy? The first American to orbit the earth was John Glenn, but who was second? (It was Scott Carpenter.) The first man to walk on the moon was Neil Armstrong, but who remembers that Buzz Aldrin was the second man to walk on the moon? Their accomplishments are important, but it's as if our brains only latch onto the memory of those who did something first.

The same is true in the Bible. We all remember the feeding of the five thousand, a miracle recorded in each of the four Gospels. But far fewer individuals remember the feeding of the four thousand, a miracle only recorded in Matthew and Mark. Had these two Gospels not recorded both miracles, no doubt some scholars would have claimed the two events were identical and that the Bible writers simply got confused when it came to the number of people present . . . or the number of leftovers collected afterward. Thankfully, Matthew and Mark record both events, so we know they are two separate accounts. But why record *two* miraculous feedings of the multitudes? What's the story behind this lesser-known miracle?

To understand the significance of this miracle, we need to follow Jesus through the land. Just before this miracle took place, both Matthew and Mark note that Jesus had withdrawn "into the district of Tyre and Sidon" (v. 21; Mark 7:31). Here Jesus encountered a Canaanite woman and healed her demon-possessed daughter. We're struck in this event by what seems to be Jesus' initial uncaring response to this woman. She cried to Him for help but He didn't answer. When the disciples told Him to send her away, He responded to them—and by extension to her—by saying "I was sent only to the lost sheep of the house of Israel" (v. 24). She then begged for help, and He answered, "It is not good to take the children's bread and throw it to the dogs" (v. 26).

We need to understand this encounter in light of Jesus' ministry to Israel. He came as Israel's Messiah, and the primary focus of His ministry was to the lost sheep of the house of Israel. This woman was a Canaanite, and as such she was not part of the covenant family of Israel. But her response demonstrated her faith in Jesus as both the Son of God and Messiah.

"Yes, Lord," she said, "but even the dogs feed on the crumbs which fall from their masters' table" (v. 27). She didn't ask that the blessing be taken from Israel; only that a small portion of that blessing be extended to her as a Gentile. In response, Jesus immediately healed her daughter. Note carefully the context. In a Gentile setting Jesus extends blessing to a woman of faith.

Matthew then says Jesus departed from there and "went along by the Sea of Galilee" (15:29). Mark provides us with a more detailed travel itinerary. "Again He went out from the region of Tyre, and came through Sidon to the Sea of Galilee, within the region of Decapolis" (Mark 7:31). Jesus traveled from the Gentile region of Tyre and Sidon to another Gentile region along the southeast side of the Sea of Galilee.

The northernmost city of the Decapolis, Hippos,

stands midway down the eastern side of the sea. The region of the Decapolis extended from there all the way down the eastern side of the Jordan Valley to present-day Amman, Jordan.

Looking across the Sea of Galilee to the Golan Heights in the region of the Decapolis

Though Jesus was by the Sea of Galilee, He was still in a Gentile region. Jesus went "up to the mountain" and the multitudes followed. Those who have been to Israel can visualize the place where this event happened. Traveling south along the eastern shore of the Sea of Galilee, visitors gaze up at an unbroken ridge of the Golan Heights just to the east of the sea. Jesus went up on this ridge, and the people followed.

At the very southeastern end of the Sea of Galilee is an area called Hamat Gader—the hot springs of Gadara. This region, with its thermal springs, was a healing center of sorts in the first century. No doubt many of those who had come there to seek out the curative properties of the hot springs heard the news about the miracle-worker in their region. Matthew records that "large crowds came to Him, bringing with them those who were lame, crippled, blind, mute, and many others, and they laid them down at His feet; and He healed them" (Matthew 15:30).

But were these people Jews or Gentiles? Matthew strongly suggests they were Gentiles. As the multitudes marveled over the healings "they glorified the God of Israel" (v. 31). This is a very unusual expression and implies that they understood the One doing the healing was doing so in the name of the *God of Israel* as opposed to the many gods worshiped in the region of the Decapolis. Jesus' amazing ministry of teaching and healing in this Gentile region continued without interruption for three days.

Jesus then announced that the disciples needed to feed the people before sending them away, "for they might faint on the way" (v. 32). In the feeding of the five thousand the disciples brought a boy who had five loaves and two fish. In this instance it appears the disciples themselves had a small supply of food with them—seven loaves of bread and a few small fish. Much like before, Jesus directed the people to be seated and then broke the loaves and fish and passed them out to the disciples who distributed them to the multitude. After everyone had eaten and were satisfied, the disciples gathered up seven large baskets filled with the pieces left over.

But we still have to ask the question, why a second miraculous feeding? Is there a deeper reason for recording this miracle? There is, and it relates to the audience being fed, and the baskets of leftovers remaining. The first miraculous feeding involved a Jewish audience and took place on the northeast side of the Sea of Galilee. It demonstrated Jesus' care for the people of Israel. He was the ultimate bread of life, and He miraculously provided for their physical needs much like God had done for Israel in the wilderness. The fact that there were twelve full baskets of leftovers hinted at God's provision for the twelve tribes of Israel—a number that implied the totality of the nation.

In contrast, the feeding of the four thousand was to a Gentile audience. Though Jesus had come to the lost sheep of the house of Israel, He also came as the lamb of God who takes away the sin of the world. He described it this way in John 10. "I have other sheep, which are not of this fold; I must bring them also" (John 10:16). Israel's

Messiah was also the light to the Gentiles. Seven is often the number of completion in the Bible, and it's fitting that in His feeding of the Gentile multitude there were seven full baskets of leftovers. He came to meet the physical—and spiritual—needs of both the Jews and the Gentiles, and the seven full baskets of leftovers show that His grace was more than sufficient.

AS WE WALK BACK DOWN THE steep slope toward the Sea of Galilee, what truths can we carry with us from these amazing days with Jesus on the Golan Heights? First, let's never forget that Jesus cares for all. He came as Israel's Messiah, and He demonstrated He could satisfy the nation's deepest physical and spiritual needs. But He also cares for all the other people of the world. No matter what your spiritual pedigree, Jesus cares for you.

Second, let's never forget that Jesus has now called on us to feed His sheep. Just as He cared for the needs of others, so He wants us to do the same. And this includes both their physical and spiritual needs. Who can you reach out to this week? As Jesus said to His disciples, "I do not wish to send them away hungry."

DAY
18

Nain

Imagine reading through the journal of a typical first-time visitor to Israel.

Day One. Our intrepid band of tourists have already visited Herod the Great's seaport of Caesarea. We saw his palace, the theater, the hippodrome, the harbor, and the aqueduct that he built to supply the city with water. We then drove to the top of Mount Carmel and relived Elijah's confrontation with the prophets of Baal. And after that we drove to the hill of ancient Megiddo—Armageddon—visiting the Canaanite high place and the ancient water tunnel while also learning about Megiddo's strategic role in history and prophecy. And now, it's time for lunch!

You might think that diary entry is just a tiny bit exaggerated, but it's not! Israel is such a small country that key biblical sites pop up every few miles. The first-time visitor can become overwhelmed, feeling like he or she is drinking from a fire hose. But don't feel bad. Mark Twain felt the same mental challenge during his visit to the Holy Land. He described the information overload this way: "How it wears a man out to have to read up to a hundred pages of history every two or three miles—for verily the celebrated localities of Palestine occur that close together. How wearily, how bewilderingly they swarm about your path!"[1] And he was slowly picking his way along rock-strewn paths on horseback. We're zipping between sites on a bus . . . over modern highways!

With Megiddo in our rearview mirror, let's drive north across the Jezreel Valley toward our lunch spot. Yet along the way there's much to see. In front of the bus, just to the right, is the Hill of Moreh with a small village just visible at its base. This town, nestled on the southern slope of the hill, is where the Old Testament town of Shunem was situated. In 2 Kings 4, Elisha the prophet raised to life the Shunammite woman's son in this town. It was an amazing miracle, but right now it's little more than a curiosity to a busload of tourists looking for lunch!

Directly in front of us is a large, modern town named Afula. It preserves the name of the biblical village that once sat here—Ophrah. Don't recognize the name? Well, it's the hometown of Gideon, the judge who defeated the Midianites with just three hundred men. Our lunch spot is just on the other side of town.

Ah, we've arrived! But before you go in to eat, let me point out just a few other locations. First, see that single, rounded hill off in the distance? That's Mount Tabor, the hill where Deborah and Barak routed the forces of Sisera. And the ridge directly in front of us is the Nazareth Ridge.

View from the Nazareth Ridge across the Jezreel Valley toward the Hill of Moreh. The village on the lower slopes of the hill is Nain.

Jesus' hometown of Nazareth is located on top. One last spot; look back at the Hill of Moreh. You're now looking at the north slope of the hill. See that village toward its base, right in the center? That's the village of Nain. I want to talk about it, but first let's get something to eat!

Wasn't lunch great! And you thought you were going to lose weight coming to Israel! But before we get on the bus, look again at the Hill of Moreh. As mountains go, Moreh is not that spectacular. The ridge is just a few miles long, and the highest peak is less than 1,700 feet high. Take note that the village of Nain is toward the base, on the north side, just below the highest peak.

Luke 7 tells us Jesus "went to a city called Nain" (v. 11). He knew the location of the village because it's clearly visible from the edge of the Nazareth Ridge where He grew up. But this is His only recorded visit to the town. This is also a singular miracle not found in the other three Gospels.

Just before this miracle Luke noted that Jesus was in Capernaum. He healed the centurion's servant there, and it must have created quite a stir. The visit to Nain took place "soon afterwards" Luke says, and Jesus was still mobbed by people attracted to this miracle worker. "His disciples were going along with Him, accompanied by a large crowd" (v. 11).

When Jesus and His band of followers arrived in Nain,

they encountered a sad scene. A "dead man was being carried out, the only son of his mother, and she was a widow" (Luke 7:12). This woman understood the heartache of death because she had already lost her husband. Now she was burying her only son. Her sorrow at his loss was compounded by her fear of the future. In Jesus' day the social security system was simple. Work hard and have lots of kids. Hopefully, enough of them will survive into adulthood to take care of you in your old age.

And that meant this woman was virtually destitute. No husband. No son. No one to care for her. She was alone and helpless. Luke then focused on a touching detail we often overlook. "And when the Lord saw her, He felt compassion for her" (v. 13). Luke reminds us that Jesus cares for the despondent, the helpless, and those who seemingly have no hope.

It's likely that others also felt compassion for this now-childless widow. But what set Jesus apart from everyone else is His divine nature. He's also the God who can change her circumstances! He walked to the pallet carrying the dead body and cried out, "Young man, I say to you, arise!" (v. 14).

As the man sat up, Jesus "gave him back to his mother" (v. 15). Few funeral processions end with the corpse crawling out of the hearse to embrace grieving family members!

We resonate with this story about Jesus' compassion and power, but we usually stop here. Look carefully at the crowd's reaction. Luke writes, "Fear gripped them all, and they began glorifying God, saying, 'A great prophet has arisen among us!' and, 'God has visited His people!'" (v. 16). Why did the crowd associate this miracle with the coming of a prophet? The answer can be found geographically. Just three miles away, on the other side of the Hill of Moreh, Elisha the prophet raised to life a woman's son. That was the greatest miracle the people in this region had ever experienced . . . until now. No wonder they saw Jesus as a prophet, and recognized that His miraculous raising of this dead son was a sign God had indeed come to visit His people.

Sadly, few scholars make this connection. Look in your Bible to see if there's a cross-reference to 2 Kings 4 or some notation comparing Jesus' miracle to Elisha's raising of the Shunammite woman's son. Some recognize the geographical connection, but many do not.

I'D LIKE US TO WALK AWAY FROM
this encounter carrying two key truths. The first truth
is the reminder of Jesus' power and compassion. He
cares for those who are hurting, and as the divine
Son of God He has the power to meet our greatest
needs. The woman had lost her one remaining means
of support, her only son. But her loss was not beyond
the comfort and power of a miracle-working God. If
you're mired in pain and heartache today, don't let go
of this truth.

The second truth is the reminder that the Bible is
about real events that happened to real people in real
places. It's no accident that two sons were raised to
life within three miles of each other. Jesus' miracle
paralleled that of Elisha, and the crowd made the
connection. The more we understand the places
where the events of the Bible took place, the more
we'll understand the Bible's message. And in the end,
our goal is to know the Word of God so we can have a
greater understanding of—and relationship with—
the God of the Word.

NOTE

1. Mark Twain, *The Innocents Abroad* (n.p.: American Publishing Company, 1869, CreateSpace/Amazon, 2010), 210.

DAY
19

Swimming
with a Millstone

Millions of us grew up playing the well-known Parker Brothers board game Clue. The game tests a player's powers of induction as he or she tries to determine the who, where, and how of Mr. Boddy's untimely death. With a mix of anticipation, trepidation, and excitement, the lucky player opens the packet of cards to determine if, indeed, the murder was committed by Colonel Mustard . . . with the candlestick . . . in the library.

Clue owes much of its success to our natural curiosity. Mysteries intrigue us. We search out the unknown, study the unfamiliar, and seek answers to the imponderable. Rudyard Kipling gently poked fun at this curiosity when he wrote:

I keep six honest serving-men
(They taught me all I knew);
Their names are What and Why and When
And How and Where and Who.

Perhaps it was such curiosity that drove the disciples to ask Jesus, "Who then is greatest in the kingdom of heaven?" (Matthew 18:1). They were certainly anxious to know what the future held. But their question was prompted by more than just idle curiosity. Each secretly thought Jesus was about to single him out and say, "Why, of course, *you* are destined to be the greatest!"

Don't be too hard on the disciples. We also long for affirmation, acceptance, and accolades. We might not be as bold as they were, but we all want to be rewarded for our effort and hard work.

Imagine their surprise when Jesus looked beyond them to a young child standing on the fringe of the crowd gathered around Him. It's possible that, just moments before, some of the disciples had pushed this very child aside as they forced their way into the center of the circle with their question. Jesus now called for the child and "set him before them" (v. 2). The child became an object lesson for these ambitious disciples.

We're very familiar with the *who* (the child) and the

what (the need for a humble faith) of this story, but we often overlook the *where*. Yet that element is crucial to the story. In Matthew 17:24, the writer placed Jesus at a specific location. "When they had come to Capernaum . . ." As a result, the events of chapter 18 likely took place in this strategic town along the shore of the Sea of Galilee. Earlier in his Gospel, Matthew described Capernaum as Jesus' "own city" (Matthew 9:1; cf. 4:13). And many of Christ's most significant miracles took place here.

But why is the location of Jesus' discussion regarding this child so significant? Because understanding the *where* of the story helps give Jesus' subsequent words greater vividness. After explaining who will be greatest in the kingdom of heaven, Jesus issued a warning to anyone seeking to cause His followers to stumble in their walk of faith. He said it would be better for them to hang a "heavy millstone" around their necks (18:6).

The two words translated "heavy millstone" are literally "millstone of a donkey." Jesus

A "heavy millstone" in Capernaum

was referring to the large, hourglass-shaped millstones turned by donkeys and used for grinding grain. Such millstones, weighing hundreds of pounds, were discovered in Capernaum and can still be seen there today.

Capernaum. The name itself is a transliteration of the Hebrew words *Kfar Nahum*—the village of Nahum. Tucked along the northwestern edge of the Sea of Galilee, the town had achieved a level of importance in Jesus' day because of its strategic location near the border of the land of Galilee ruled by Herod Antipas. Less than three miles away the Jordan River separated Herod Antipas's kingdom from that ruled by Herod Philip. The Romans saw the strategic importance of the town. That's why they posted a garrison of soldiers and established a tax collection office there.

But for the common laborer in Capernaum, life revolved around the lake and the fertile soil along its shores. Fishing must have been the primary occupation, but the dark volcanic rock in the area had weathered into a rich soil that made farming an attractive option. The Jewish historian Josephus put it this way. "The land is everywhere so rich in soil and pasturage and produces such variety of trees, that the laziest are tempted by these facilities to devote themselves to agriculture. In fact, every inch of the soil has been cultivated by the inhabitants" (Josephus, *Wars* 3.3.2). Little wonder that Capernaum had such an abundance of millstones for grinding grain. And that brings us back to Jesus' words to His disciples.

Jesus said it would be better for an individual to tie a large, heavy millstone around his neck and be "drowned in the depth of the sea" than to cause one of His followers to sin. Again, location is everything. Jesus spoke these words as He stood beside the Sea of Galilee. It's easy to visualize Jesus pointing to one of the many millstones being turned by donkeys in the area and then, in a sweeping gesture, turning and pointing toward the Sea of Galilee.

It's as if Jesus said, "You want to put a snare or trap in the way of My young followers to trip them up? I've got a suggestion that will actually be more beneficial for you. See that large basalt millstone over there? Take a rope and fasten the millstone around your neck. Then drag it over to the Sea of Galilee and jump in! Bringing about your own physical death would be better for you than the eternal judgment you will receive from Me for harming My children."

ARE YOU A CHILD OF GOD?

Have you put your faith in Jesus Christ as your personal Savior? If so, then don't miss the reality of what Jesus is saying. He cares for you! But how can this truth help you today?

Many people go through life angry over past wrongs done to them, harboring bitterness, reliving hurtful scenes over and over in their minds. Others look for ways to settle scores and repay those who have scarred them physically or emotionally. Such anger and bitterness are parasites that suck joy from life and rob us of peace and contentment. Perhaps you are struggling with such burdens today. If so, think carefully about Jesus' words.

He cares for His children. He knows when they are mistreated. And someday He will judge those who have harmed His followers. I can release my anger and bitterness because God has promised to watch over me. There will be consequences for actions, but they'll happen in accord with His timetable, not mine.

If I'm wronged, I can choose to harbor hatred. But I pay a heavy physical and emotional price for bearing that burden. The millstone at Capernaum is a reminder that God will bring about justice in His own time. I just need to trust Him.

DAY 20

Does God Help Those Who Help Themselves?

According to researcher George Barna, eight out of ten Americans believe that the statement "God helps those who help themselves" is found in the Bible, which, of course, is not true. Versions of the statement can be traced all the way back to Aesop—six centuries before the time of Christ. The statement as we know it was popularized in America when Benjamin Franklin first published it in his *Poor Richard's Almanack.*

But why do so many think it's found in the Bible? I think it's primarily because it sounds like other pithy statements found in the Bible. And besides, it just sounds so . . . so . . . so *American*! In a country that has historically honored self-reliance, we assume such a virtue must have the blessing of almighty God.

The Bible does stress personal accountability and individual responsibility, but it does *not* present self-reliance as a virtue. In fact, just the opposite is true. Proverbs 28:26 says, "He who trusts in his own heart is a fool." Proverbs 3:5 exhorts us to "trust in the LORD with all your heart and do not lean on your own understanding." The problem with self-reliance is that it can result in the prideful belief that, as the poem "Invictus" suggests, we are the masters of our fate and the captains of our souls—which is *not* true.

And maybe that's why the miracle in John 5 makes us feel just a little uneasy The apostle tells us Jesus was in Jerusalem for one of the annual Jewish feasts, and John draws our attention to one particular location. "Now there is in Jerusalem by the sheep gate a pool, which is called in Hebrew Bethesda, having five porticoes" (v. 2).

We can visit a portion of this pool today, located about a hundred yards inside St. Stephen's Gate, next to St. Anne's church. The name *Bethesda* means "house of mercy," and John says the pool had five covered porches or walkways. Archaeologists have helped verify John's description. The pool was surrounded on four sides by these porches, and a fifth extended across a dam in the middle that divided the pool into two halves. The pool itself was up to forty feet deep, and the two sections of the pool together held about sixteen million gallons of water.

In a part of the world where water means life, the pool must have been impressive. Certainly that much water was a visible reminder of God's mercy. Yet the scene that unfolds is anything but merciful! John writes that the entire area was a sea of human suffering. "In these lay a multitude of those who were sick, blind, lame, and withered" (v. 3a).

At this point there's a bit of controversy over whether the next statement is actually part of what John wrote. Why is there a problem? Listen to the next two verses. The in-

The Pool of Bethesda in the model at Jerusalem

firm were "waiting for the moving of the waters; for an angel of the Lord went down at certain seasons into the pool and stirred up the water; whoever then first, after the stirring up of the water, stepped in was made well from whatever disease with which he was afflicted" (vv. 3b–4).

In other words, these verses seem to say God helps those who help themselves! The waters began moving and the first to drag himself into the water got healed. With the depth of the pool, it makes me wonder what happened to the *second* person into the water—someone who was also disabled, but who *wasn't* healed!

I think you see why people have a problem with these verses. It sounds as though God is willing to heal the person with the least amount of disability—or the greatest amount of outside assistance—while the most needy and helpless are left in their pitiful state.

And yet, I believe these verses are part of the original text. So how do I reconcile what was happening here with the character of our God? I do so by challenging one assumption. We assume that the "angel of the Lord" who stirred the pool was a good angel. But we know from Scripture that a third of the heavenly angels joined with Satan in his initial rebellion against God. What if the angel stirring up the waters was one of the *fallen* angels? I believe real healings did occur at the pool, but those healings came through the actions of a fallen angel, not from the hand of God.

Holding people captive to such false hopes has Satan's fingerprints all over it. About a hundred years after the time of Christ a temple was built at this site to Asclepius, the Greek god of healing. Why build a healing center here? Perhaps because healings had indeed taken place here—but not from the hand of God.

Satan tries to duplicate God's power and implies people can earn favor by their own deeds. In contrast, Jesus demonstrates the true healing power of God. In verse 5 He approaches one of the most hopeless of those packed into the area, "who had been ill for thirty-eight years." Jesus' question to the man was direct. "Do you wish to get well?"

The man explains his pitiful plight. He has no one to assist him when the waters are stirred. "While I am coming, another steps down before me" (v. 7). He is too disabled to make it to the waters first. Yet, it seems as if this is his only hope for healing, so he has remained captive to the pool for most of his life.

In contrast to the fickle promise of healing associated with the pool, Jesus demonstrates the true healing power of God. In verse 8, He commands, "Get up, pick up your pallet and walk." God's healing is instantaneous and comes through no effort on the part of the man. "Immediately the man became well, and picked up his pallet and began to walk" (v. 9).

But verse 9 says there was a problem. "Now it was the Sabbath on that day." Since the Pool of Bethesda was just to the north of the temple, it doesn't take long for the man to be spotted by some of the religious leaders on their way to worship, and they accost him for violating the Sabbath. The scene is almost comical.

The man has just been miraculously healed. (That doesn't seem to register with these leaders.) The healing takes place at a spot that might very well have demonic overtones. (That's not a problem to these leaders.) The man is walking home carrying the mat on which he has been confined for years, and it happens to be Saturday, the Sabbath. (And *that* is the key issue for these leaders.)

It becomes obvious through their conversation with the man that he had no idea who had healed him. In the initial excitement, as the man stood up and cried out to those around him that he had been healed, Jesus had slipped away.

Eventually the man makes his way to the temple, and in verse 14 that's where Jesus finds him. Look carefully at what Jesus says. The phrase "Behold, you have become well" might suggest the man had also been well sometime in the past. Jesus then tells him, "Do not sin anymore, so that nothing worse happens to you." Perhaps the man's original paralysis was the result of some past action on his part. Jesus now warns him to stop sinning or an even worse fate awaits him, probably a reference to God's eternal judgment.

HERE ARE TWO MORE LESSONS

from our time with Jesus at the Pool of Bethesda. Each is directed to a different group. First, to those who choose to deliberately disobey God, Jesus says there are consequences to our actions. God didn't give rules to choke off fun. But like a good parent, He did set boundaries for our own protection. There's a price to pay for exceeding those boundaries. That price can be short-term heartache and physical pain. And, sadly, such actions can also have eternal consequences.

The second lesson is directed to those who might be smiling and thinking they are specially blessed by God because they *do* follow all His rules. But be careful that you don't substitute *rule-following* for a true *relationship* with God. The religious leaders were so intent on making sure no one carried a mat on the Sabbath that they failed to notice the spiritually destructive activities taking place just to the north of the temple. The Christian life is ultimately about a relationship with Jesus. It can't be reduced to just keeping a list of rules.

God *doesn't* help those who help themselves, but He *does* extend mercy to the helpless, and He *does* seek to establish a deep, intimate relationship with those who claim to follow Him.

DAY 21

When Jesus Celebrated Hanukkah

anukkah is the eight-day Jewish holiday about which Christians seem to know so little. Perhaps it's because we're so preoccupied with Christmas, the celebration of Christ's birth that falls about the same time—and which, in its commercialized form, seems to scream for attention the entire month of December. Or perhaps it's because Hanukkah isn't found in the Old Testament. The festival came into existence during the intertestamental period as a result of the Jewish struggle against Antiochus Epiphanes following his desecration of the temple in Jerusalem.

Those not familiar with the writings of Josephus or 1 Maccabees probably don't know the details of this epic struggle for the very survival of the Jewish faith. It's a story

Christians ought to know, because it's a reminder of God's faithfulness to the descendants of Abraham, Isaac, and Jacob even during dark days of persecution. The eight-day festival commemorates the rededication of the temple in Jerusalem following its three-year desecration as a pagan shrine. Here's the end of the story as it's told in 1 Maccabees:

> For eight days they celebrated the rededication of the altar. With great joy they brought burnt offerings and offered fellowship offerings and thank offerings. . . . Now that the Jews had removed the shame which the Gentiles had brought, they held a great celebration. Then Judas, his brothers, and the entire community of Israel decreed that the rededication of the altar should be celebrated with a festival of joy and gladness at the same time each year, beginning on the twenty-fifth of the month of Kislev and lasting for eight days (1 Maccabees 4:56–59).[1]

Great story. But what does the celebration of Hanukkah have to do with Jesus, and with you? The answer might surprise you.

In the Jewish calendar, the months are determined by the moon. The first sliver of a new moon marks the beginning of the month. The lunar months are then realigned with our 365-day solar year by adding a thirteenth month to the calendar every few years. As a result, Jewish holidays seem to change dates on our calendar, though they always fall within the same general period of time. Hanukkah was to begin on the twenty-fifth day of Kislev. That month generally falls between mid-November and mid-December, so Hanukkah usually begins around mid-December, just prior to our celebration of Christmas.

Jerusalem is a beautiful city, but late December is not always the best time to visit. December through February are the coldest—and rainiest—months of the year. In December, the average temperature ranges from the low 40s at night to the mid 50s during the day, and nearly four-and-a-half inches of rain will fall, with almost every other day seeing some measurable rainfall. The days can be dark, damp, and dreary. And if there's a cold, biting wind pushing in from off the Mediterranean, you can quickly become chilled to the bone. Now, there can also be some beautiful sunny days in December, but they are not commonplace.

Perhaps God chose the dark, cold days of December as a backdrop to display His faithfulness to His people and His covenant. What a wonderful time to celebrate a feast of lights and dedication—to remember God's faithfulness during an earlier time of spiritual darkness.

And that's why, in John 10, we find Jesus in Jerusalem

during Hanukkah. "At that time the Feast of Dedication took place at Jerusalem; it was winter, and Jesus was walking in the temple in the portico of Solomon" (vv. 22–23). Most pass by this verse without stopping, but note John's attention to detail. He identifies the specific feast—it was the Feast of Dedication, which we now call Hanukkah. He identifies the time of the year—it was winter, mid- to late-December on our calendar. And he identifies the specific location where the events that followed took place—in the temple, in an area called the portico of Solomon, or

Close-up of the portico of Solomon in the model of the second temple

Solomon's Colonnade.

The portico of Solomon wasn't built by King Solomon. His temple had been destroyed nearly six centuries earlier. But the large, covered area on the southern end of Herod's rebuilt temple was so magnificent that the people associated it with the great achievements of Solomon in the past. This same covered area is later mentioned in Acts 3:11 and 5:12. The area was a veritable forest of limestone columns reaching skyward to support the roof that stretched out above, offering shelter to the throngs gathered below.

Why note that Jesus is walking in this colonnaded area? We don't know for sure. Perhaps the events that follow took place on one of those cold, damp, rainy days that come in December.

Maybe the crowds are heavier than normal under the colonnade because of the driving rain falling on the exposed courtyard surrounding the temple itself. The people are cold and slightly damp from the walk to the temple, and their mood seems to match the weather—foul and blustery. Their patience with Jesus has worn thin, and they come immediately to the point. "How long will You keep us in suspense? If you are the Christ, tell us plainly" (John 10:24).

That seems like a reasonable request . . . until you realize that Jesus throughout His ministry *had* revealed His identity. He told Nicodemus He was the Son of God (John 3:16); He told the woman at the well He was the Messiah (John 4:25–26); He told the religious leaders He would summon the dead back to life for judgment and that He was the one predicted by Moses (John 5:45–47). He challenged the crowd to believe in Him and announced that He existed *before* the time of Abraham (John 8:56–58).

The problem isn't His lack of clarity; it's their lack of faith. "I told you," Jesus announces, "and you do not believe" (John 10:25). And that brings us to the heart of the issue. Hanukkah is the Feast of Dedication, celebrating the time when the temple was rededicated to the service of God. It's also known as the Feast of Lights to commemorate the lighting of the menorah. And yet during this very festival the people are in spiritual darkness because they refuse to put their trust in the true "Light of the world" (John 9:5). They seek to seize the One who had Himself earlier cleansed the temple (John 2:13–25) because He doesn't fit their conceptions of the promised Messiah.

THIS CONFRONTATION WITH JESUS at Hanukkah offers two lessons for you and me. The first is that Jesus' miracles validate His claim to be Israel's promised Messiah. "The works that I do in My Father's name, these testify of Me. . . . If I do not do the works of My Father, do not believe Me; but if I do them, though you do not believe Me, believe the works" (John 10:25, 37–38). The many miracles Jesus performed while on earth confirm His claim to be God's Son—and Israel's Messiah!

The second lesson is that Jesus offers to protect those who put their faith in Him. "My sheep hear My voice, and I know them, and they follow Me; and I give eternal life to them, and they will never perish; and no one will snatch them out of My hand. My Father, who has given them to Me, is greater than all; and no one is able to snatch them out of the Father's hand. I and the Father are one" (John 10:27–30). Jesus' miracles demonstrated God's power, and that same power is the basis for our hope of eternal life.

On a dark, dreary December day Jesus stood in the temple and offered the assurance of eternal life to all who would come to His light. No matter what the future holds, nothing is more powerful than the clasped hands of God the Father and God the Son. You *cannot* be pried from their grasp!

NOTE

1. Good News Translation (Today's English Version, second edition) copyright © 1992 American Bible Society. All rights reserved.

DAY 22

Blind Bart and The Two Jerichos

I grew up watching the old-time Westerns on television. Roy Rogers. The Cisco Kid. Hopalong Cassidy. Maverick. Cheyenne. I loved them all. My friends and I would gallop our way through the neighborhood with our six-shooter cap guns, blasting away at the imaginary bad guys and all the other assorted hombres who had the misfortune of meeting up with our posse.

As I think back on all those Westerns, I especially remember the colorful nicknames given to the cowboys, sidekicks, and their female friends. *Bat* Masterson. *Hopalong* Cassidy. *Gabby* Hayes. *Kitty* Russell. Those nicknames seemed to capture the essence of the character being portrayed on the screen. But what does the Old West—and colorful nicknames—have to do with the

Bible? Well, today we're traveling to Jericho to visit with a man who, had he lived in the Wild West, would likely have been called "Blind Bart."

Blind Bart was a beggar who tried to collect from those going from Jericho . . . to Jericho. No double talk here. There's Old Testament Jericho and New Testament (Roman) Jericho. The original city of Jericho was built next to a powerful spring known today as Elisha's Spring or Sultan's Spring. This unfailing spring, the largest in the lower Jordan Valley, provided the life-giving water that allowed the city to flourish in a barren region.

But Herod had a problem with this sunny city that abounded with date palm trees. The original city had a large Jewish population, and Herod had a rather tense relationship with the subjects he governed. The location was superb, but the neighbors could be disagreeable.

So Herod worked out an ingenious solution.

About a mile from the site of Old Testament Jericho Herod built a new city—Roman administrative Jericho. It lacked the water supply of the original city, so Herod built an aqueduct to bring water from a spring in the Judean Wilderness several miles away. He built a palace for himself straddling the streambed at the edge of the mountains. His palace complex included a swimming pool, where he later murdered his own brother-in-law, whom he saw as a threat to his rule. And just above the entire complex stood the fortress of Cypros, a well-defended refuge should Herod ever feel threatened by his nearby subjects.

Like Minneapolis and St. Paul, or Dallas and Fort Worth, the two cities of Jericho were separate yet inextricably linked together. And once we recognize this fact, the story of Blind Bart makes more sense.

As our story begins we're walking with Jesus from Jericho . . . to Jericho. Matthew says Jesus' encounter with Blind Bart took place as Jesus and His disciples were *"leav-*

View from Old Testament Jericho toward the Roman-administered Jericho, located at the base of the hill in the distance

ing from Jericho" (20:29). But Luke says the event took place as Jesus "*was approaching* Jericho" (18:35, italics added). So did Jesus meet Blind Bart as He was coming *out* of Jericho or going *into* Jericho? In reality, both statements are correct. Matthew, writing to a Jewish audience, reported that Jesus encountered Blind Bart as He was leaving Old Testament Jewish Jericho, while Luke noted He met the man as He was approaching Roman administrative Jericho.

Mark's account supports this understanding. He writes that Jesus and His disciples "came to Jericho," referring to Old Testament Jericho. Mark then notes that Jesus encountered the beggar "as He was *leaving* [Old Testament] Jericho" (Mark 10:46). Blind Bart had strategically positioned himself along the roadway connecting the two towns.

Mark also tells us the man's name. Blind Bart was, in reality, Bartimaeus, which he translates as the "son of Timaeus." Blind Bart's name seems to match his location. That is, it appears to be a mixture of the Aramaic word *bar*, which means "son," and the Greek word *timaios*, which means "honorable." So here was a man with a mixed Jewish/Gentile name sitting along a road connecting cities with separate Jewish and Roman cultures.

But if his name means "son of honor," his life had fallen far short of the aspirations of his parents at birth. He had been reduced to the lowest status of society, "sitting by the road begging" (Luke 18:35). Matthew actually tells us that there were two beggars sitting there, but evidently Bartimaeus was the more outspoken of the two. Mark and Luke both turn their spotlight on him.

Blind Bart heard the large throng of people heading his way as they left Old Testament Jericho on their way toward New Testament Jericho and the road that went past it to Jerusalem. While most beggars would have used the opportunity to call out to everyone passing by, Bartimaeus focused with laser-like precision on one specific person in the crowd. "Jesus, Son of David, have mercy on me!" (Mark 10:47).

How did he know about Jesus? Mark tells us that he heard that it was "Jesus the Nazarene" who was about to pass by. And it's likely he had heard stories about Jesus' miracles, and perhaps His teaching. But Blind Bart's words—and his persistence—tell us he had a greater depth of insight about Jesus than most of those in the crowd.

Two phrases stand out in his cry for help. First, he recognized that Jesus was the "Son of David." This is more than just a genealogical reference to Jesus being from the tribe of Judah. He was acknowledging that Jesus was the Messiah. Matthew records that during Jesus' triumphal entry into Jerusalem on Palm Sunday the crowd shouted the same thing. "Hosanna to the Son of David; blessed is he who comes in the name of the Lord!" (Matthew 21:9). With 20/20 spiritual insight, Blind Bart shouted out, "Jesus, you are the Messiah!"

His second phrase captured the essence of what he wanted from his Messiah. "Have mercy on me!" It's almost certain that the word he shouted out came from the Hebrew word *hesed*, a word that means "unmerited favor" or "loyal love." He was asking Jesus to extend His gracious help to someone who possessed nothing of value to justify it. Such mercy is based on the inherent goodness of the One giving the help, not the worthiness of the one receiving it.

The crowd rebuked Bart and told him to be quiet, but he cried out all the more. And that's when Jesus stopped and summoned him. "What do you want Me to do for you?" Jesus asked. "Rabboni, I want to regain my sight" was his simple response (Mark 10:51). And Jesus then announced, "Go; your faith has made you well" (v. 52). Blind Bart was blind no more.

THIS ENCOUNTER ALONG THE
dusty road connecting the two cities of Jericho offers, appropriately, two key lessons. First, it reminds us that we all begin life spiritually blind, and our blindness can only be removed when we recognize that Jesus is the Son of God, the promised Messiah. Our spiritual healing must be based on His mercy alone. That's the reality to which Blind Bart clings.

There's nothing we can do to heal ourselves. Have you come to the point in your life where you have acknowledged that you need God's mercy for your spiritual healing? Jesus died on the cross to pay the penalty for your sin. If you call out to Him, He will extend His mercy and forgiveness.

Second, Bartimaeus's response to God's mercy offers a lesson in commitment. After receiving his sight, Mark said Bartimaeus "began following Him along the road." If you've experienced God's forgiveness, have you committed to wholeheartedly follow Jesus along life's road? There is no better path you can follow! Just ask the man once known as Blind Bart!

DAY
23

Shorty in the Sycamore

In the area where I grew up, people often gave others nicknames based on their occupation, physical characteristics, or family relationships. No matter how old I get, some of the "senior saints" in the church there still call me "Little Charlie."

I got a chuckle out of reading football coach Bobby Bowden's autobiography, *Called to Coach*. Writing about his time at South Georgia College in the mid fifties, he said, "It seemed like every one of my players had some sort of nickname." He then goes on to tell about Bull, Stumpy, Ape, Blinkey, Doodlebug, Tiny, and Reverend. Those guys would have felt right at home in my hometown!

Nicknames were also used in the time of Jesus, though

we only know a few of them. We call Thomas the disciple "Doubting Thomas," but that wasn't his nickname. John 11:16 tells us that people called him Didymus—the word for "twin." Evidently Thomas had a twin brother, so people called him "the twin." And I almost feel sorry for the second Simon in the list of disciples. Everyone knows Simon Peter, but what about the other one? He's known as "Simon who was called the Zealot" (Luke 6:15). How would you have liked to go through life being known as "the fanatic"? The nickname could have been given because of Simon's religious zeal or because Simon was a member of the Zealot party, a political group bent on overthrowing the Roman government. If it's the latter, it would have described this zealot's focus *before* he met the Messiah, Jesus.

There's another individual in the New Testament who might also have had a nickname. But if he did, it probably wasn't said to his face. He was too rich and powerful for that. I'm talking about Zaccheus. If he had grown up in my hometown, he probably would have been called Shorty.

Jesus' encounter with Shorty took place in the spring, and the temperature in Jericho is pleasant that time of year—upper 60s at night, climbing to a delightful mid 80s during the day. Jericho only receives four to six inches of rain each year, but it remains a thriving oasis because of the powerful springs of water nearby. It was the Palm Springs of Judea.

At the time of Jesus, Jericho was divided into two centers. The Jewish city was still located near the hill on which Old Testament Jericho had once stood. This area was fed by a large spring that breaks to the surface right at the base of the hill. About a mile away Herod the Great built a palace that straddled a ravine carving its way out of the Judean Wilderness. He built an aqueduct to bring water from a spring in the wilderness to meet the needs of his new Jericho. A Roman administrative center grew up around this new site.

But back to Shorty . . . I mean, Zaccheus. I suspect his parents wondered where they had gone wrong. His name comes from the Hebrew word *zaccai,* which means "pure," "righteous," "clean," or "innocent." That likely described the hope his parents had for him when he was born, but Zaccheus chose a different path in life—one despised by most Jews. Luke tells us he had become a "chief tax collector" (v. 2).

People in the United States complain about the Internal Revenue Service, but there's little comparison between Zaccheus and someone working for the IRS today. Zaccheus worked for a foreign occupying power, Rome. Tax collectors were usually wealthy individuals who "bought" the right to collect the taxes. This authority allowed them to extort additional funds for themselves—

A sycamore-fig tree in Jericho

the equivalent of legally sanctioned robbery. Zaccheus was a wealthy man, and at least some of his wealth came by collaborating with the Romans against his own people.

Many recall the children's song about the "wee little man" who "climbed up in a sycamore tree" to see Jesus. But few have actually seen a sycamore-fig tree like the one in the biblical account. Sycamores in Israel aren't like a typical American sycamore tree. The variety in Israel grows fairly tall, and the trees produce a small, fig-like fruit that grows on the trunk and branches. It would have been relatively easy for Zaccheus to climb into a sycamore-fig tree, and its foliage could have helped hide this man who wanted to see—but not necessarily be seen.

Imagine Zaccheus's surprise when, reaching the spot where he was perched, Jesus stopped, looked up, and said, "Zaccheus, hurry and come down, for today I must stay at your house" (Luke 19:5).

Luke draws a contrast between Zaccheus and the crowd following Jesus. The crowd surrounded Jesus, so much so that Zaccheus couldn't get near Him. But when Jesus announced His intention to go as a guest to Zaccheus's house, the crowd started muttering. "He has gone to be the guest of a man who is a sinner" (v. 7).

To understand the story, we need to look back one chapter to Jesus' parable of the Pharisee and the tax collector in Luke 18. The Pharisee represented those who thought they were righteous because of what they do for God. The tax collector represented those who acknowledged their own sinfulness and humbly sought God's mercy.

Now one chapter later we come face-to-face with the real-life characters from the story. Zaccheus the tax collector, seeing Jesus, accepted the Lord's offer to fellowship with him, acknowledged his past wrongs, and sought to realign his life to match the character of God. And as a result, Jesus said to him, "Today salvation has come to this house. . . . For the Son of Man has come to seek and to save that which was lost" (Luke 19:9–10). Make no mistake. Zaccheus had indeed been lost, but through this encounter he found new life in Christ.

Sadly, the crowd never got it. They compared themselves to Zaccheus, and felt superior. Like the Pharisee in Jesus' parable, by exalting themselves and judging others, they never discovered God's true forgiveness for their sins. They wanted to be seen crowding near the Rabbi, but they never got close enough spiritually to understand His heart.

Thankfully, Zaccheus did. And the encounter changed his life. Though he disappeared from the biblical record after this encounter, later church tradition suggests Zaccheus continued to follow Christ. A fourth-century writing called the *Apostolic Constitutions* identified "Zaccheus the tax collector" as the first bishop of the church at Caesarea. While we don't know if the story is true, it's at least possible that Zaccheus left his position as chief tax collector to become a devoted follower of Christ, and a leader in one of the early churches in Judea.

AFTER THIS ENCOUNTER,

Zaccheus might have remained a "wee little man" physically. But God transformed him into a spiritual giant among those living in Jericho. And that's, perhaps, the best lesson we can take with us as we watch Jesus and Zaccheus walk toward Zaccheus' home. God knows your heart, and He *will* reveal Himself to you if you truly want to see Him. It doesn't matter who you are or what you might have done. Today, right now, look in faith toward Jesus. Place your trust in Him as your Savior and Lord. He wants to come to your house today!

DAY 24

The Tearful, Triumphal Entry

My dad has always carried a pack of Wint O Green Life Savers in his pocket. He was the self-appointed candy man at our church. And when little kids walked up and asked for a Life Saver, he would first ask them to quote a Bible verse. John 3:16 was a constant favorite, but a close second was John 11:35, "Jesus wept"— the shortest verse in the English Bible. Two words could get you a Life Saver!

That verse, as short as it is, gives us great insight into the character and compassion of Jesus. MacArthur captures the incredible depth of meaning found in this tiny sentence as he describes the word used for weeping—a word used only here in the New Testament. "In contrast to the loud, wailing implied by *klaio, dakruo* has the connotation of silently bursting into tears, unlike the typical funeral mourners. Jesus' tears were generated both by His love for Lazarus and by His grief over the deadly and incessant effects of sin in a fallen world."[1]

But this is *not* the only time we find Jesus weeping. Come with me as we follow Jesus on His journey over the Mount of Olives into Jerusalem on Palm Sunday.

We begin, amazingly enough, at the village of Bethany were Jesus wept over the grave of Lazarus, just a few short months earlier. As the crow flies, we're just a mile-and-a-half from Jerusalem—but before we're done we might wish we were a crow. The road from Bethany to the top of the Mount of Olives is very steep.

After just a few hundred yards our calf muscles are beginning to tighten up, and our breathing is becoming labored. And it dawns on us that most of the artistic representations of Jesus have it all wrong. He was no wimp! We're struggling to keep up as Jesus and His disciples stride quickly up the road.

Suddenly, two disciples pick up the pace, half-walking, half-running to the village a few hundred yards ahead, and we hear the report rippling back through the crowd. "Jesus sent them ahead into the village. He said they'd find a colt tied there, and He asked them to untie it and bring it back for Him." Some in the crowd wonder if perhaps Jesus Himself is getting tired. But no, Jesus is about to fulfill a prophecy by Zechariah about Israel's Messiah. "Rejoice greatly, O daughter of Zion! Shout in triumph, O daughter of Jerusalem! Behold, your king is coming to you; He is just and endowed with salvation, humble and mounted on a donkey, even on a colt, the foal of a donkey" (Zechariah 9:9).

Jesus knows a colt will be tied up and waiting! And His decision to ride into Jerusalem on that colt is not for His benefit but for the benefit of those in Jerusalem. It is a sign that identifies Him as the Messiah, the promised King!

The colt arrives. Some of the disciples remove their coats and place them across the back of the colt for a makeshift saddle. Still other disciples begin throwing their coats across the pathway, forming a carpeted walkway for this royal procession. As we get closer to the summit of the Mount of Olives the crowd swells in size. Some follow the lead of the disciples, throwing their coats across the road. Others strip palm branches from nearby trees, hoping to blanket the pathway in a carpet of green.

The joyous procession takes on a life of its own as it begins the descent down the Mount of Olives toward Jerusalem. You're no longer out of breath, but you still must pay close attention to the roadway. The palm branches are hiding both rocks and ruts in the road. Meanwhile the colt seems oblivious to the obstacles as it picks it ways down the hillside carrying its royal passen-

Walking down the Mount of Olives with the walls of Jerusalem in the distance

ger on its back.

The crowd has grown into a massive throng. Someone starts quoting Psalm 118—a psalm looking forward to the coming of the Messiah—and soon the whole throng seems to be shouting it in unison. "Blessed is the King who comes in the name of the Lord; peace in heaven and glory in the highest!" (Luke 19:38; cf. Psalm 118:26).

You push your way forward, finally catching up to Jesus. You turn to look into His face, to make eye contact, to connect with Him in a way that allows you to share in this incredible time of celebration and triumph by seeing it all through His eyes.

And you discover Jesus is sobbing uncontrollably. Luke describes the scene this way. "When He approached Jerusalem, He saw the city and wept over it, saying, 'If you had known in this day, even you, the things which make for peace! But now they have been hidden from your eyes'" (19:41–42). The word for weeping that Luke chose is not the one used to describe Jesus in John 11:35, the one that pictured gentle tears streaming down His face. The word used by Luke points to uncontrollable sobs of sorrow.

But why is Jesus weeping while everyone else is so excited?

Jesus is crying because, as God, He knew the hearts of the people . . . and He knew the future. In just five days this same crowd now welcoming Him as King would shout to Pilate, "Crucify Him . . . We have no king but Caesar." Jesus could also see the coming destruction of Jerusalem that would take place "because you did not recognize the time of your visitation" (Luke 19:44).

The surging crowd snaps you back to reality. The people are passing you on their way down the mountain. They are so wrapped up in the moment they haven't even bothered to look into the eyes of the One they are supposedly honoring. They are so busy celebrating the coming of the miracle worker that they fail to notice His tears and sobs.

Matthew tells us that just two days after this event Jesus will deliver a final lament over the city. "Jerusalem, Jerusalem, who kills the prophets and stones those who are sent to her! How often I wanted to gather your children together, the way a hen gathers her chicks under her wings, and you were unwilling. Behold, your house is being left to you desolate! For I say to you, from now on you will not see Me until you say, 'Blessed is He who comes in the name of the Lord!' " (Matthew 23:37–39).

IT'S TIME FOR US TO HEAD BACK.

But what lessons can we take back with us from this journey with Jesus over the Mount of Olives? Here are two. First, we catch a glimpse of Jesus' humanity and His deity. As a man, He wept over the death of a friend and the rejection of a city. But as God He called that friend back from death to life; as God He announced to the city what would take place five days—and thirty-five years—in the future: His crucifixion and Jerusalem's destruction.

Second, we learn there are two times when Psalm 118 ("Blessed is He who comes in the name of the LORD!") is applied directly to Jesus. One is past and the other is future. The words were first shouted by the multitude on the Mount of Olives on Palm Sunday. Sadly, the events of the next few days show that the crowd didn't really mean them. But Jesus said there will come a time when the words of Psalm 118 will be shouted aloud again by the people of Jerusalem. He was referring to His second coming, that time when His feet will again stand on the Mount of Olives as He comes to rescue and save His chosen people.

The first Palm Sunday was a time of sorrow for Jesus. It launched a series of events that led to His death on the cross to pay the penalty for our sin. But there's another "Palm Sunday" in the future—a second triumphal entry into Jerusalem that will happen at His second coming. And this time, Jesus will not be weeping!

NOTE

1. John MacArthur, *John 1–11*, The MacArthur New Testament Commentary (Chicago: Moody, 2006), 466.

Jesus Cleanses
the Temple

I love books! The shelves in my office are filled with a jumble of old classics, commentaries, and reference works. And over time, the books have started filling the space between the shelves. It wasn't always that way. Back when I had a much smaller collection, I kept them organized by topics, using simple, stamped-metal bookends to hold the partially filled shelves of books in place. But two sets of gift bookends were special because they were gifts from friends. One set was made of blown glass and the other of marble, and they added a sense of elegance to the books in between. Those bookends highlighted some of the more prized collections of books in my library.

In the same way, there are two nearly identical incidents in the Bible that help bookend and set apart the ministry of Jesus. I'm referring to His two cleansings of the temple. John 2 describes a time at the beginning of His ministry when Jesus cleared the temple, while Matthew, Mark, and Luke describe a similar event that took place the week before His crucifixion. Let's visit the temple during both incidents.

In John 2 Jesus visited Jerusalem just after performing His first miracle. When He arrived in Jerusalem for Passover, "He found in the temple those who were selling oxen and sheep and doves, and the money changers seated at their tables" (v. 14).

To understand this scene, we need to know Jewish Passover customs. During Passover each family was to bring a Passover lamb to be sacrificed on the temple altar. People coming to Jerusalem from a great distance had a problem because the lamb they were to bring had to be without blemish or defect, and there was the possibility their lamb could get injured during the journey.

Jewish custom solved this problem. People could bring money to Jerusalem and purchase a Passover lamb there. But where could one purchase such a lamb? The normal place would have been outside the temple. But where there's an opportunity to make a profit, there also exists the temptation for abuse.

We don't know how it began, but clever vendors had

moved their wares into the temple, probably into the Court of the Gentiles. Perhaps the temple priests simply chose to ignore this infraction or, more likely, they were profiting by selling the concession rights to the vendors or even controlling the business themselves. But in any case, the temple livestock market was open for business! The bleating of sheep and lowing of cattle mixed with the prayers of the people inside the temple precincts.

Near the cattle pens were the tables of the money

The entire temple complex in the model of the second temple in Jerusalem

changers. God required Jewish men to pay a half-shekel temple tax. And the leadership decreed it had to be paid using one particular coin. If you didn't have that coin, you could exchange the coins you did have for the proper currency—for a fee, of course!

Business was brisk this Passover season when Jesus showed up in the temple to begin His one-man cattle drive. Fashioning a whip from cords, He drove the animals out of the temple. Picture the scene. Worshipers on their way up the stairway to the temple jumped to the side and pressed themselves against the cold limestone walls as a mixed throng of young lambs and calves skittered their way down the steps.

Jesus then turned to face the tables of the money changers. Sweeping His hand across the tabletops, He scattered the coins, then grabbed the tables and overturned them. I imagine the money changers momentarily jumped back—and then scurried forward to scoop up the coins bouncing across the stone plaza. As the disciples watched this drama unfold, the words of Psalm 69:9 came to mind. "Zeal for Your house has consumed me."

The cleansing of the temple in John 2 is bookended by a similar scene in the Synoptic Gospels that occurred the week of Jesus' crucifixion. It's likely the temple leadership did remove the offensive practices from the temple for a while in response to Jesus' first demonstration.

But the financial incentives were just too great, and some of the activities found their way back into the temple courts. Lambs and calves were no longer being sold there, but caged doves were permitted, as were the money changers.

The second confrontation in the temple occurred during Jesus' final week of ministry. According to Mark's account, one day after His triumphal entry into Jerusalem, Jesus "entered the temple and began to drive out those who were buying and selling in the temple, and overturned the tables of the money changers and the seats of those who were selling doves" (11:15). I can picture the latches on the wooden cages of the doves popping open, the cages clattering to the stone floor as the birds take flight, swooping around the court in their race toward freedom. And the coins of the money changers once again rolled and bounced their way across the plaza. Total pandemonium!

Mark also added that Jesus "would not permit anyone to carry merchandise through the temple" (Mark 11:16). The word translated "merchandise" is actually the word for a vessel, jar, or dish. Most likely, it refers to people carrying jars of water or other products. It's not necessarily that they were selling these items on the Temple Mount. More likely, they were simply using the temple as a shortcut across the city. That makes perfect sense.

Whether traveling north to south or east to west, visitors would find the broad, flat expanse of the Court of the Gentiles a tempting shortcut, allowing someone to avoid the narrow streets winding through the rest of the city.

The Mishnah prohibited individuals from entering the Temple Mount with their staff, sandals, or wallet, and it also prohibited them from using the temple as a shortcut. But people were disregarding these prohibitions; that is, until Jesus became "The Enforcer."

All these activities must have been taking place in the Court of the Gentiles, the large plaza surrounding the inner court and temple proper. This was the closest place those who weren't Jewish were allowed to get to the God of Israel. In Isaiah 49:6, God commanded Israel to be "a light of the nations so that My salvation may reach to the end of the earth." As a result, in Isaiah 56:6–7, God described a time when "foreigners" would come to His "holy mountain" so that the house of God "will be called a house of prayer for all the peoples." But in Jesus' day the place of prayer for the Gentiles had been converted into an open-air market where vendors took advantage of those coming to worship God. Or, as Jesus said, these hucksters had made it "a robbers' den" (Mark 11:17).

TWO LESSONS ARE CLEAR FROM Jesus' two cleansings of the temple. First, in our informal, secular, almost profane society, we need to remember that God is holy and that He is worthy of our sincere reverence and respect. The Bible says the "fear of the Lord is the beginning of knowledge" (Proverbs 1:7), but we seem to have lost that profound sense of reverential awe. Jesus is calling on us to give God the honor due His name.

Second, Jesus is reminding us that we have also been called to serve as lights to the world. And so we need to ask ourselves this disturbing question: Do our words and deeds point people toward the awesome God of the universe, or is our casualness toward God sending the message that He's not really worthy of our respect and devotion? Does Jesus need to cleanse the temples of our lives . . . so others see God's glory radiating out from us?

The traditional Upper Room on Mount Zion

DAY
26

The Upper Room

The traditional Upper Room in Jerusalem epitomizes *everything* that is confusing about a pilgrimage to the Holy Land. For example, Jesus told His two disciples to "go into the city" and meet a man carrying a pitcher of water who would lead them to the owner of a house with a large upper room (Mark 14:13–15). But the Upper Room people visit today is *outside* the walls of the Old City. And it sits directly above the tomb of David. It's hard to envision Jesus having His Last Supper in a room just above a tomb. But don't worry. The traditional tomb of David is actually on the wrong hill!

Confused yet? Well, it gets worse. You climb the stairs and walk into the Upper Room, only to discover the arched ceiling dates back to the time of the Crusades—

a thousand years *after* the time of Jesus! (Check out the photo on page 208.) And the entire room had at one time been turned into a mosque. It's hard to picture Jesus seated in front of the *mihrab*, the niche in the wall that indicates the direction of Mecca.

Your guide begins to speak, and you discover the final flaw in this Upper Room. The stone floor, walls, and ceiling give new meaning to the term "reverberation." Every whisper and cough bounces off the walls and ceilings to form a noisy rumble that makes it almost impossible to identify a distinct human voice. If Jesus had delivered His message in *this* Upper Room, the disciples would have had no idea what He said!

But don't get too discouraged. While the traditional Upper Room is not *the* room where Jesus met with His disciples, it's at least located in the right part of town. In Jesus' day the area was inside the city walls and would have been filled with large houses that had spacious upper rooms. We might not be at the actual Upper Room, but we're on the right hill!

When most of us think of the Last Supper, Leonardo da Vinci's painting comes to mind. Like a scene from a covered-dish supper at church, we picture a long table filled with plates, bowls, and cups. Jesus is seated in the center with the disciples crowded around to His left and right. Unfortunately, da Vinci's painting reveals more about fifteenth century Italy than it does about the celebration of Passover in the time of Jesus. So let's go back and look at the real events of the Last Supper.

The table in the original room is not a traditional dining table with chairs. Rather, it's a very low U-shaped table (but with the horseshoe curve in the table squared off), with cushions on the floor around the three outer sides. The guests recline around the table on the cushions, resting on their left elbow with their feet extending away from the table.

Because of da Vinci's famous painting, we expect Jesus to recline on the very center cushion, with the disciples fanning out on both sides. But instead, Jesus walks to the upper-right side of the U-shaped table, reclining at the second spot from the end. This was the normal spot where the host reclined. He would then invite two honored guests to recline to his right and left. We wait to see whom Jesus has chosen to honor.

The apostle John goes to the upper-right side of the table and reclines at the very top position, immediately to the right of Jesus. As he leans on his left elbow, he's almost leaning against Jesus Himself. No surprise here because John was one of the three disciples most closely identified with Jesus. But who will take the other position of honor? Surely it's got to be Peter or James, the other two disciples in the inner circle.

As observers, we're surprised at who climbs onto the cushion just to the left of Jesus. It's Judas Iscariot, the other disciple whom Jesus has chosen to honor on this special night. But since Judas is the treasurer for the group, some of the others think Jesus might be honoring him for his faithfulness in that capacity.

It also becomes obvious that Peter is offended at not being offered a place of honor. Rather than selecting a cushion close to Jesus and those Jesus has chosen to honor, Peter deliberately stomps to the opposite end of the U-shaped table—the position of least honor. It's almost as if he's trying to make a statement about his displeasure by choosing the seat farthest from the host. The other disciples take their seats, and the Last Supper is set to begin.

I suspect that about now you are saying to yourself, *Wait a minute! How do we know the location of John, Judas, and Peter at the Last Supper?* That's a fair question, so let's look at the details that help us establish these facts.

Matthew 26:20 describes the beginning of the Last Supper. "Now when evening came, Jesus was reclining at the table with the twelve disciples."

Knowing that everyone is reclining helps us identify the position of the apostle John. John refers to himself in his Gospel as "the disciple whom Jesus loved" (13:23; 20:2; 21:7, 20). And in John 13:23–25 he tells us where he was reclining when Jesus announced that one of the Twelve was about to betray Him. "There was reclining on Jesus' bosom one of His disciples, whom Jesus loved" (v. 23). So John was next to Jesus. But on which side? "He, leaning back thus on Jesus' bosom, said to Him, 'Lord, who is it?'" (v. 25). The custom of the day was to recline on one's left elbow while eating with the right hand. In this position, John *had* to be located just to the right of Jesus, at the very end of the table. Only from that position could he lean back against Jesus.

And that leads us to the position of Judas at this final meal. How do we know where Judas was reclining? John 13 also seems to provide the answer. After Jesus announced that one of the Twelve would betray Him, John leaned back and quietly said to Jesus, "Lord, who is it?" (v. 25). Jesus must have whispered the answer to John. The betrayer was to be "the one for whom I shall dip the morsel and give it to him" (v. 26). Then Jesus dipped the bread and handed it to Judas. For this to take place, Judas must have been seated next to Jesus.

Okay, but how do we know where Peter was reclining? Well, Peter had to be positioned where he could make eye contact with John. Just after Jesus announced that one of the Twelve would betray Him, Peter "gestured" to John to have him ask Jesus to identify the person (v. 24). This makes most sense if Peter was at the opposite end of the U-shaped table, directly across from John. From here he could get John's attention and encourage John to ask Jesus.

AS WE STEP FROM THE ROOM,

what can we take away from this time with them? Perhaps it's the reality that we don't need to visit a room built during the Crusades over the supposed tomb of David to believe the truth of the Bible. The biblical account of the Last Supper is so accurate in its details that we can reconstruct the very spots where Jesus and the key disciples were reclining at the table. And knowing I can trust the Bible for the smallest of details assures me that I can also trust what it says about life's most important issues.

What are you struggling with today? Look back to the Upper Room and see how accurately God preserved all the physical details of that scene. God also preserved the words Jesus spoke that night, and they contain a message of hope for you. "Do not let your heart be troubled; believe in God, believe also in Me" (14:1). Pause today and read the rest of John 14. And discover for yourself Jesus' words of hope from the Upper Room!

Old olive trees in the Garden of Gethsemane

DAY 27

The Three Gethsemanes

A visit to Gethsemane requires us to stop at the three locations for the site. Why three locations? This isn't a case of different religious groups each claiming to know the *exact* spot of Gethsemane. Rather, it's an opportunity for us to explore three separate spots that merge together the night Jesus was betrayed.

Our first stop is, literally, at the very bottom of the Mount of Olives. Watch yourself as we cross the street and head down this flight of stairs to the open plaza area below. Take the narrow alleyway to the right of the small building ahead and walk to the small entrance at the end.

Step through the door and down the handful of steps into the relatively small chapel. You are now at Gethsemane! Look carefully at the walls and ceiling. Take away the lights, the seats, and the other modern additions, and it's not too hard to recognize that we're in a cave. It's a natural cave, like hundreds of others that can be found in the limestone hills throughout Israel. But what's Gethsemane doing in a cave?

The name "Gethsemane" is actually a combination of two Hebrew words—*gath*, which refers to a press, and *shemen*, which is the word for olive oil. When Jesus went with His disciples to Gethsemane, He was literally going to the olive oil press. But why are we standing in a cave?

Olives are harvested at the very end of summer, just as the rainy season is about to begin. To guard against water getting mixed in with the oil, presses were often placed in some type of enclosure like a building or a cave. Here on the Mount of Olives this natural cave was the perfect location for a press. And during the rest of the year the cave served as a convenient shelter or gathering point for those visiting Jerusalem, especially during the festivals. Very likely, Jesus and His disciples used this cave for shelter during past visits. On the night of His betrayal Jesus "proceeded as was His custom to the Mount of Olives," and, with His disciples, "arrived at the *place*" (Luke 22:39–40, italics added). The group, minus Judas, came to the cave with its olive oil press. No doubt the disciples assumed this would be the spot where they would bed down for the evening since it was too late to walk all the way to Bethany.

I know we would all like to pause here for a while, but we need to keep moving—to the second of our stops at Gethsemane.

The second spot is the traditional Garden of Gethsemane that most tourists visit. Outside the cave, where the olive press was, we should expect to find olive trees. (And we're standing at the base of the Mount of *Olives*, after all.) At the time of Jesus, a "garden" would have referred to a cultivated area—a working agricultural farm, not a flower garden. So somewhere near the press we ought to find an olive grove. How near? Luke tells us Jesus went about a stone's throw away from the other disciples.

How far is it from Gethsemane—the olive oil press in the cave—to the traditional Garden of Gethsemane? Depending on how good an arm you have, I'd say it's about a stone's throw away! So as we enter the garden to look at the gnarled olive trees, realize we are somewhere near the spot where Jesus must have separated from the rest of the disciples, taking with Him Peter, James, and John.

As we look at these trees, picture Jesus standing among them with the three disciples who formed His inner circle. What were His instructions to these three? "Keep watching and praying that you may not enter into temptation; the spirit is willing, but the flesh is weak" (Matthew 26:41). And what was their response? They fell asleep! Three times! I can almost picture Peter propped up against a tree very similar to one of these, snoring softly. But don't be too hard on these disciples. It was late at night. It was dark. And they had just finished eating the Passover seder.

Right beside this small grove of olive trees is a modern church. This is one of my favorite churches in all the Holy Land. The Church of All Nations includes several highlights by architect Antonio Barluzzi within the structure. The windows are made from translucent purple alabaster. They allow some light to enter, but they block enough to make the interior of the church seem dark and somber. And the bedrock is exposed intentionally at the front of the church. It marks the spot where Jesus went by Himself to pray.

Barluzzi's distinctive church is the third location on our tour of Gethsemane. The Gospel of Mark says that Jesus went "a little beyond" the three disciples before falling to the ground to pray (14:35). Somewhere in this area—perhaps at the very spot we see at the front of the church—is the location where Jesus wrestled with the reality of the coming horror of His crucifixion. As He agonized in prayer, Luke records that His sweat became like drops of blood, an indication of the deep emotion Jesus was experiencing. "Father, if You are willing, remove this cup from Me; yet not My will, but Yours be done" (Luke 22:42).

I'm not allowed to guide inside the church, but here's what I would like you to do. Take a seat and pause to think about the emotions Jesus felt that night. For all eternity God the Father and God the Son had been in perfect unity. But Jesus was now about to be crucified. And as He hung on the cross He would cry, "My God, My God, why have You forsaken Me?" (Matthew 27:46).

Jesus knew that the moment He took on Himself the sin of the world He would experience not just the horrific pain of physical crucifixion. He would also experience all the separation, judgment, and punishment required for our sins by God the Father. Is it any wonder that as He prayed that night He was in agony? Yet, in the end, Jesus was willing to submit to it all because of His great love for you.

AS WE WALK OUT OF THE CHURCH and into the bright sunlight, it's time for application. Reflect on the immense significance of this location. This is where Jesus agonized in prayer over the personal cost required of Him to pay for our sins. Look at the photo of the olive trees in the garden (page 216) and picture Jesus waking up His slumbering disciples to go back to the olive oil press in the cave. There He would meet Judas and the mob from the chief priests and elders—and begin the sequence of events that would lead to the cross.

But before we leave this hallowed spot, may I ask you one last time about life's most important question? Have you placed your trust in Jesus as your personal Savior? He died on the cross to pay the penalty for your sin, and He did so willingly because of His love for you. You can receive Him today by praying to God and saying something as simple as, "Dear God, I know I've done wrong. I believe Jesus died on the cross to pay the penalty for my sin, and I now want to open my heart and receive Him as my Savior. Please forgive me of my sin and have Jesus take control of my life."

If you make that decision today, please let us know. We would love to help you understand more about this new life that you just began. Contact me by e-mail at thelandandthebook@moody.edu or write to me at The Land and the Book, 820 N. LaSalle Blvd., Chicago, IL 60610.

The Garden Tomb in Jerusalem

DAY 28

The Road to Calvary

Inside the ancient city of Jerusalem, the sun's harsh rays reflect off the limestone walls, its brilliant light washing the color out of the scene and giving the city the black-and-white look of an old photograph. And yet, in spite of the blazing heat, the streets are alive with activity.

A group of pilgrims—wearing brightly colored hats that mark them as tourists—snake their way down the traditional *Via Dolorosa*, the "Way of Sorrow" traveled by Jesus on His final journey to Calvary. They walk carefully down the stone-paved street, its limestone blocks worn to a slippery smoothness. Every few yards they must step around a puddle of water or pile of garbage, leftover reminders that people still live and work in the houses and shops that crowd against the street on each side.

Trying to ignore these distractions, the pilgrims attempt to focus on the incredible events that unfolded in this tiny city twenty centuries ago. They want to experience what it was like during that Passover when the Lamb of God was slain for the sins of the world. They try to imagine the physical pain felt by our Lord, the anguish and fear of His followers, the harsh shouts of the guards marching the condemned prisoners to the place of death.

But the cries of vendors calling from shops shatter the sacred moment. "Twenty postcards. One dollar!" "Hand-carved olivewood crosses!" "You're my first customer. I'll make you a special deal!" Any last hope for pious reflection is shattered when the group finds the *Via Dolorosa* temporarily blocked by a Coca-Cola truck making deliveries!

At first glance, this commercialism seems to mock the sacredness of the site. But as is so often the case in the Middle East, the profane hawking of religious trinkets is probably closer to the reality of the day Jesus hung on the cross than the sacred veil we try to drape over the event.

The day the soldiers marched Jesus through the streets of Jerusalem, the streets were also lined with vendors hoping for a profitable holiday shopping season. They shouted at those passing by to "stop and shop" at their store. They offered the latest in lamps, oil, cloth, leather, and other items needed by pilgrims coming to worship at the temple.

Perhaps the vendors paused briefly as several condemned criminals were shoved down the street, the wooden beams of their crosses lashed to their shoulders. Most likely, shopkeepers and shoppers alike retreated into the stores, not wanting to block the way, or attract the attention, of those brutal soldiers. But scarcely had the grotesque parade passed when the stores reopened and the bargaining began anew.

What was the day of Christ's crucifixion really like? Jesus was not the quiet, impassive Savior carrying the t-shaped cross while dressed in white. He was bruised and bloody, caked with dirt and stained with sweat. The crossbeam He carried was coarse, rough-hewn, splintered. It was the work of a soldier, not a craftsman. Its purpose was utilitarian, not aesthetic. It represented death. Crosses today are too symmetrical, too polished and shiny—too perfect. They are more decoration than declaration, more fashion statement than faith.

And Jesus didn't carry His cross to a grass-covered "hill far away." The place of crucifixion stood outside the gate, along the road, so those traveling by could see the ugly horror of capital punishment and think twice about defying the government of Rome. The authorities intended for the accusation posted over the head of the condemned to be read by those passing by—so they would know why the individual had to die.

This was also a time to practice a crude form of "victim's rights." Those who had been harmed by the condemned individual could now vent their anger and derision. They could mock, curse, and even spit on the one who had caused them such pain and grief in the past. At Jesus' crucifixion it was the religious leaders who rejoiced over His pain and suffering.

And yet then, as now, most simply chose to ignore Christ's crucifixion. Maybe they were too busy shopping, cleaning, cooking, or preparing for Passover to notice the brutal parade or to hear the hammer blows as iron nails pushed through human flesh and embedded in wood. Others perhaps knew—and even were troubled—by the events of that day, but they were too afraid or distracted or apathetic to do anything. For whatever reason, the crowd that gathered around the cross was largely composed of religious leaders and Roman soldiers. Only a few of His followers dared to gather and watch.

Before that day ended, Jesus' lifeless body was pulled from the cross and handed to Joseph of Arimathea for a hasty burial. The sun was setting, Passover was at hand, and it was no time for the smell of death to permeate the homes of Jerusalem. Jesus died amid two thieves, but He was buried in the new grave of a wealthy man. And yet even in death He was the subject of controversy. The religious leaders remembered His promise to rise from the dead, and they asked the Romans to seal and guard the grave.

But Sunday morning brought the declaration of Jesus' victory over sin and death! God shattered the stillness of the early morning, shook the earth, rolled away the stone, and posted His own angelic guards to make sure all who came knew that "He is not here, for He has risen just as he said" (Matthew 28:6).

My favorite spot in Jerusalem is not the *Via Dolorosa*, or the Church of the Holy Sepulchre, or even the hill often called Gordon's Calvary. These are special, they are meaningful, and they're haunting in the spiritual hold they've had on generations of pilgrims. But the spot that excites me most is the Garden Tomb and the simple sign that hangs on its door. It reads, "He is not here—for He is risen." We don't worship the grave . . . we worship the Son of God who arose from the grave! Places are important because they remind us of the reality of the events that occurred there. But always remember, our hope rests in a living Savior, not a cold slab of limestone that once served as the temporary resting place for His human body.

OVER TWO CENTURIES AGO ISAAC
Watts pondered the death and resurrection of Christ,
and the response we as believers should have to
such an incredible act of love. Read—and reflect
on—the words he penned in "At the Cross."

Alas, and did my Savior bleed?
And did my Sov'reign die?
Would He devote that sacred head
For such a worm as I?

Was it for crimes that I had done
He groaned upon the tree?
Amazing pity! grace unknown!
And love beyond degree!

But drops of grief can ne'er repay
The debt of love I owe;
Here, Lord, I give myself away—
'Tis all that I can do.

At the cross, at the cross where I first saw the light,
And the burden of my heart rolled away,
It was there by faith I received my sight,
And now I am happy all the day!

Sign identifying the entrance to Emmaus

The Road
to Emmaus

Even the simplest statement can be incomprehensible if you don't understand its historical or cultural context. Here's an example from my background growing up on the edge of the anthracite coal region in northeastern Pennsylvania. Imagine overhearing the following conversation: "What da ya think they're chargin' for mangoes?" "About a buck two-eighty." "I'll bet it's a lot, heyna?"

Now, you probably thought you just overheard two people suggesting that a fruit, called a mango, would cost about $3.80 at the local grocery store. In reality, the first person asked how much a bell pepper would cost, and the second said he wasn't sure of the exact price. The first person then responded by saying it would be expensive, and sought affirmation of that fact. It's simple . . . once you know that a bell pepper in that area is called a "mango," a "buck two-eighty" means an unknown amount of money, and "heyna" means "isn't that so?"

Sometimes we feel the same way about God's Word. We know it must make sense, but we can't seem to figure it out. If you've struggled to understand the Bible, don't be discouraged. Sometimes we need to learn more about the historical background before we can understand it. And that's where a good Bible teacher can be helpful. When a gifted teacher opens the Word of God, it's as if a spotlight comes on, and the words of the Bible make sense.

That's why I would love to have attended the Bible study that took place on the road to Emmaus. Only two disciples showed up for the study, and they were discouraged. But everything was about to change because the Bible teacher that day was Jesus.

The two disciples were traveling from Jerusalem to the village of Emmaus. While most Bible translations say the town was "about seven miles from Jerusalem," there is a textual issue. Depending on which Greek manuscript is used, the distance was either sixty stadia (seven miles) or one-hundred sixty stadia (eighteen miles). I believe the longer distance is probably correct. I say this because there was a town named Emmaus located in the Aijalon Valley, about eighteen miles from Jerusalem, at the time of Jesus.

Traveling to Emmaus in Jesus' day was not a simple journey. The two disciples would have walked north from Jerusalem for several miles before turning west at Ramah. Their route would connect the hill country of Judah with the Aijalon Valley. Walking at a normal pace, the journey would have taken about five hours.

As the two disciples walked along, they discussed the bewildering events of the past few days. Soon they were joined by a third person they didn't recognize. "What are these words that you are exchanging with one another as you are walking?" he asked (Luke 24:17). They stopped and looked down, sadness and disappointment reflected in their faces and in their voices. Was this stranger only a casual visitor to Jerusalem who hadn't heard about the remarkable events that had happened there over the past few days?

The man pressed them for details, so they told him about Jesus. He was "a prophet mighty in deed and word in the sight of God and all the people, and how the chief priests and our rulers delivered Him to the sentence of death, and crucified Him. But we were hoping that it was He who was going to redeem Israel" (vv. 19–21). Their hoped-for Messiah had died. But the situation had taken an unexpected twist that very morning, the third day since His death. "But also some women among us amazed us. When they were at the tomb early in the morning, and did not find His body, they came, saying that they had also seen a vision of angels who said that He was alive. Some of those who were with us went to the tomb and found it just exactly as the women also had said; but Him they did not see" (vv. 22–24).

The response of the stranger must have startled them. "O foolish men and slow of heart to believe in all that the prophets have spoken! Was it not necessary for the Christ to suffer these things and to enter into His glory?" (vv. 25–26). It's as if this stranger not only knew what had taken place, He knew *why* it had happened. He rebuked the two disciples for not recognizing that the recent events had been predicted in the Old Testament. "Then beginning with Moses and with all the prophets, He explained to them the things concerning Himself in all the Scriptures" (v. 27).

Think about those words for a second. He begins His Bible study with "Moses," meaning the first five books of the Bible. And He continues from there through "all the prophets," explaining how God had predicted the Messiah's sacrificial death and resurrection.

If Jesus appeared early during the men's journey, they would have been with him several hours. Imagine, a five-hour Bible study with Jesus! What passages would He have taught?

What about God's message to the serpent in Genesis

3:15? "He shall bruise you on the head, and you shall bruise him on the heel." This was God's first promise to destroy the Evil One, even though the serpent would strike at the heel of the promised Deliverer.

Perhaps He quoted Psalm 16 where David declared, "My body also will rest secure, because you will not abandon me to the grave, nor will you let your Holy One see decay" (vv. 9–10 NIV). David couldn't have been simply describing himself because his grave was still in Jerusalem. His body did see decay. But the body of the "Holy One" predicted by David wouldn't see decay.

I'm sure Jesus went to Isaiah 53. The Messiah had to die, to be "pierced through for our transgressions," "crushed for our iniquities," and to have had "the iniquity of us all" laid on Him. He would be "cut off out of the land of the living" for the sins of the people and "His grave was assigned with wicked men, yet He was with a rich man in His death" (vv. 5–6, 8–9). The Messiah had to die a sacrificial death to pay for the sin of the world, be buried . . . and *then* live again!

He also must have taken them to Zechariah 12. When the Messiah descends to the Mount of Olives in triumph, "they will look on Me whom they have pierced" (v. 10). Only *after* He had been pierced would He return as King.

Eventually, the three reached Emmaus. The disciples urged the stranger to stay because it was "nearly evening:

the day is almost over" (Luke 24:29 NIV). He went to their home for a meal. Then "He took the bread and blessed it, and breaking it, He began giving it to them" (v. 30). And then their eyes were opened and they realized the stranger was Jesus Himself! At that instant He vanished from their midst.

As the sun sank into the Mediterranean to the west, these two disciples rushed back toward Jerusalem, a return hike of eighteen miles and five more hours! Their excitement kept them moving. It was likely almost midnight before they finally arrived back at the home where the other disciples were gathered.

THEIR MOBILE BIBLE STUDY

offers us at least two lessons. First, we learn anew that the Bible is a book about Jesus. From beginning to end the book points to Him.

Second, God *is* at work, even when we don't understand what is happening. Even during loss and pain. These disciples longed for the ruling Messiah, but they didn't realize the suffering Messiah had to arrive first. They got the crown ahead of the cross, and they had become discouraged when events didn't turn out as they had hoped. But the confusion was theirs, not God's. And when we're confronted with events we don't understand, we need to trust Him to work out the details.

Just ask the two disciples from Emmaus!

Ancient mosaic on the church floor at Tabgha

DAY
30

A Fish Fry
with Jesus

I am *not* a fish person. When I take groups to Israel and we stop at the Sea of Galilee for a St. Peter's fish lunch, I'm the guy ordering St. Peter's pizza instead! But I still find John 21 fascinating. It's the first and only fish fry in the Bible. Let's stop by for a visit . . . and you can have my fish!

The story opens by the Sea of Galilee as the first rays of the sun begin to creep above the mountains to the east. Fishing was done at night, so it's now time for the fishermen to head to shore, dry and repair their nets, and then get some well-deserved rest. But the fishermen out on the lake this morning are disappointed. It's been a wasted night of fishing. The apostle John—one of those in the boat—tells us "they caught nothing" (v. 3).

Following His resurrection, Jesus had commanded the disciples to go to Galilee and await His arrival. The anticipation was too much for someone like Peter, who needed to be *doing* something instead of just sitting around. That's when he announced to the others, "I am going fishing" (John 21:3), and they followed his lead.

Now it is morning. Time to quit, despite not catching a single fish. As the disciples prepare to stow the nets and row toward home, they are interrupted by a shout from shore. "Children, you do not have any fish, do you?" (v. 5). Perhaps it is a merchant seeking to buy their catch. Their answer would be sure to disappoint him. "No," they shout back.

But instead of turning away, the stranger shouts again, "Cast the net on the right-hand side of the boat, and you will find a catch" (v. 6). They are about a hundred yards from shore. How could He see a school of fish on the other side of the boat? Yet he speaks with such confidence— and they have done so poorly up till now—that they decide to give it a try. Besides, there is something about the voice of this stranger that just seems familiar and trustworthy.

That one final cast of the net makes up for the entire night. The net encloses a school of fish so large that "they were not able to haul it in" (v. 6). And at that point it all clicks with the apostle John. He looks at Peter and says simply, "It is the Lord" (v. 7). The voice. The sure command. The amazing results. It reminds John of an earlier encounter on these shores—another miraculous catch of fish that had taken two boats to haul to shore (Luke 5:1–7).

John's confirming word is all it takes to convince Peter who, in true Peter-like manner, immediately jumps overboard and started swimming to shore!

Where did all this happen? Almost certainly it took place somewhere along the northern shore of the Sea of Galilee. Bethsaida and Capernaum are in that area, and that's where these disciples had grown up fishing. Along the shore, just a little southwest of Capernaum, is a spot where seven springs of water flow into the Sea of Galilee. These warm springs attract fish—and the spot must have been known to veteran fishermen, including the disciples. That place, called Tabgha today, could be the spot where Jesus first met the disciples, and it's also a good possible location for this meeting in John 21.

But let's go back to our story.

When Peter and the disciples reach the shore, they see "a charcoal fire already laid and fish placed on it, and bread" (John 21:9). They had worked all night, and Jesus had already anticipated their physical needs. To me, the most intriguing part of the story comes right now. Jesus calls to the disciples and says, "Bring some of the fish which you have now caught." Think about this. Jesus already had fish cooking over the fire. Where did they come from? We are not told but it's possible He simply created them. Couldn't He have created more? He had multiplied five loaves and two small fish into a meal large enough to feed five thousand men, as well as their wives and children. Couldn't He multiply the fish already cooking into a meal large enough to feed this small band of disciples?

He could, and that's why I find His command so fascinating. I believe that, having arrived on shore and realizing it is Jesus, the disciples have already forgotten about the fish. In fact, the fish are still in the net—still in the water! In asking them to bring some of the catch for the meal, Jesus is redirecting their attention to the first amazing miracle of the day. Peter climbs back on board the ship and single-handedly pulls the net filled with fish the rest of the way to shore.

John then adds a detail that demonstrates he was an eyewitness to the event. He notes the net contained 153 fish—an exceptionally large catch—and yet the net had not broken (v. 11). Why 153 fish? People have tried to find some deep, spiritual meaning in that number, but I like John MacArthur's answer. "The simple, obvious explanation, however, is that this was the actual number of fish they had caught."[1] That is, the number has no significance beyond the fact that Jesus had enabled the disciples to catch a *mess* of fish!

Think about that for a second. The disciples are confused and uncertain. Jesus had died, then rose from the dead and spoke to them (John 20:19–23). But they still don't know what this means for them. And they are in Galilee without Him, uncertain of what the future holds. Peter defaults to what he knows best—fishing—and the other disciples follow his lead. By going fishing, he's going back to the one activity where he feels comfortable and secure.

PERHAPS THE MOST IMPORTANT lesson for the disciples that morning—and for us today—is that Jesus is still watching out for them. *He* arranges for the catch of fish. *He* keeps the nets from breaking. *He* already has a meal prepared for them when they reach shore. He may soon leave them, but He is not abandoning them. He will meet their needs in ways they couldn't even begin to imagine.

There's a second lesson for the disciples and for us: Focus on the priorities. Time management expert Steven Covey has expressed the lesson this way: "The main thing is to keep the main thing the main thing." Jesus emphasizes this truth to His disciples by switching from fishing to shepherding. Having shown that He could be trusted to meet their needs, He now turns to ask whether they can be trusted to focus on the mission. Peter had taken the lead among the disciples in coming to Jesus, so Jesus singles out Peter to answer this most important question. "Simon, son of John, do you love Me more than these?" (John 21:15).

For many years I imagined Jesus was asking if Simon loved Him more than he loved the other disciples. But in context I think Jesus is asking if Simon loves Him more than those things that had given Simon satisfaction and security in the past. Simon knows fishing, and this is Simon's default occupation when life seems to unravel. His words, "I'm going fishing," begin John 21. In essence Jesus has just shown that He'll continue to care for His disciples. But now He wants to know if they care for Him more than those things that had been at the center of their lives in the past. If Peter's love for Jesus exceeded his love for fishing, then he is to demonstrate it by taking care of Jesus' followers, pictured as helpless sheep. Jesus could be trusted to care for His disciples. Now He asks if they can be trusted to care for those who will become His followers.

And this is where we have to say good-bye to the disciples and to this amazing fish fry by the Sea of Galilee. But Jesus' question still lingers in our ears. Do *you* love Jesus more than those things that were once the center of your life? If so, how do you demonstrate it? It's as simple as reaching out to meet the needs of others as you trust in God to meet your needs.

NOTE

1. John MacArthur, *John 12–21*, The MacArthur New Testament Commentary (Chicago: Moody, 2008), 394.